DOES A WILD BEAR CHIP IN THE WOODS?

Lewis Grizzard

ON GOLF

Published by
LONGSTREET PRESS. INC
2150 Newmarket Parkway
Suite 102
Marietta, Georgia 30067

Printed in the United States of America
94 93 92 91 5 4

Library of Congress catalog Card Number: 89-63793

ISBN 0-929264-25-8

This book was printed by R. R. Donnelley & Sons, Harrisonburg, Virginia. the text was set in Century Schoolbook by Typo-Repro Service, Inc., Atlanta, Georgia. Cover photographs by Joe Benton Photography. Illustrations by David Boyd.

DEDICATION

To all those golfers who hit 'em like they live . . .
low and hard.

Contents

DOES A WILD BEAR CHIP IN THE WOODS?

What It Was Was Golf

The reason I'll probably never shoot par, nor dare to shoot under it, is because I come from a golf-deprived background. (I also come from a yacht-deprived background, a tell-Charles-to-saddle-my-horse and a Europe-for-the-summer-deprived background, but this is a golf book, so I won't bore you with stories about turning over in a boat in Mud Lake, about my grandfather's mule "Daisy," or about the fact that the first time I went to Europe, it was with my third wife.)

I grew up in Moreland, Georgia, a town of three hundred people about forty miles southwest of Atlanta. There was no such thing as the Moreland Country Club. We had Steve Smith's Truck Stop where you could play the pinball machine or go in the restroom and buy a twenty-five-cent condom, which was an exercise in futility, given the fact nobody had sex in Moreland until the middle seventies.

Not only was there no golf course in Moreland, I also

grew up with a negative attitude about golf. That is because my grandfather (I lived with my mother and her parents in my formative years) saw golf as what was wrong with this country between 1952 and 1960.

He was a Roosevelt Democrat who relived the Depression every day. When my grandfather read newspaper accounts or saw television reports of President Eisenhower taking a few days off to golf at Augusta National, it angered him.

"Angered" really isn't the correct word here. It was more like his face would turn red, his blood pressure would go up and his hands would shake and he would say, "That Republican son of a bitch ought to get off the golf course and get back to Washington where he belongs. That's what's wrong with this country."

In addition to my grandfather's dislike for Ike's golfing habits, it seemed disdain for golf and for golfers was universal in the low-income South in those days.

Golf was pasture pool. Golf was a sissy game. Bankers played golf, and everybody hated bankers. Golf was the game of the idle rich, who had all the money and wouldn't give any of it away.

Because of this background, I turned to other sports, such as baseball, a very cheap sport. All you needed was a ball, which could be covered with electrical tape and used for years after its original hide wore off, a bat, and a few gloves to swap around when one team came into the bat and the other went out to the field.

While those who didn't come from a golf-deprived background were out on the practice range at their snobby country clubs learning to keep their heads down and their right elbows in, I was swinging at a ball of black tape with a baseball bat while wearing a pair of black, high-top U.S. Keds, the poor, distant cousin to the Foot-joy.

I firmly believe that, with very few exceptions, you can never be a low handicap golfer if you were out playing baseball when you were a kid and didn't get a chance to learn the proper golf swing and how to sign a club ticket. The problem was that I didn't know all that at the time, and when the opportunity did arise for me to take up golf, I didn't know it probably was too late, and I would never really know how not to "come over the top," a golf term meaning hitting the ball left into a swamp, or "blocking out," a golf term for hitting the ball right into a condominium.

But, at sixteen, when I took my first official rip at the golf ball, I didn't know a lot of other things, either, such as there are no answers in the bottom of a glass, never take the Denver Broncos in a Super Bowl no matter how many points they are getting, and just because a woman says, "I love you," it doesn't mean she won't take your car, your house and your stereo when she runs off with some blond stud on the mini-tour.

Three things happened to get me started in golf when I was sixteen:

(1) My grandfather died. I don't think he would have ever forgiven me if I had taken up golf during his lifetime, and I loved that old man.

(2) I got my driver's license when I was sixteen. I was suddenly mobile.

(3) Mr. Brown opened a golf course four miles from my house.

Actually Mr. Brown didn't open a golf course at all. He opened what he *called* a golf course, the Brown Bell Golf Course in scenic Turin, Georgia. (Turin is near Senoia, which is an old Indian word for "triple bogey.")

Mr. Brown had some land. There was an old house and a barn on the land. He dug nine small holes (I presume with a post-hole digger, which you need when you are building a fence or burying a small dog), put poles with flags in the holes and had instant golf course.

The old house became the clubhouse. You teed off on the first hole down near the barn.

It cost seventy-five cents to play nine holes, $1.25 to play eighteen. That included a pull cart. If you wanted to ride, you could rent Mr. Brown's John Deere tractor for a slightly higher fee.

When I heard about Mr. Brown's golf course, I immediately decided to take up golf. I drove to the hardware store in the county seat of Newnan. (Newnan had a country club. Nobody from the country could afford to join, however.)

I purchased a set of Chandler Harper golf clubs. In case you don't remember Chandler Harper, he probably doesn't remember you either.

My set included a driver, three-wood, a three-, five-, seven- and nine-irons, a pitching wedge and a putter. The set cost me $29.95, which is what a sleeve of Slazenger Belata balls costs today. I didn't have a bag. What did I need bag for? I carried my clubs on my shoulder.

The very next day, I drove over to Mr. Brown's golf course, paid my seventy-five cents for nine holes, bought three used Club Special golf balls for a quarter each, walked down to the barn, teed up one of my Club Specials, and my golf career began right there.

I had seen some golf on television. First, you put the head of the club down near the ball and just stood there. The ball wasn't going anywhere until you hit it, so if you wanted to stand there a half an hour, you could. I stood there about three minutes, thinking, "Wasn't Chandler Harper Millard Fillmore's vice president?"

What you did after that was take the club back and hit a line drive to centerfield.

The first golf shot I ever made was a foul ball into the seats behind first base. Strike one.

My second shot was a swing and a miss. This guy had a helluva curve ball. My third shot was a dribbler to the mound.

The good thing about golf, I reasoned at that point, was even if you hit a dribbler to the mound, you were still at bat.

I probably made a fourteen on my first hole of golf. I've seen high-handicap women golfers reach the green in twenty-six and plumb-bob their putts. At least I didn't plumb-bob my putts on my first golf hole ever. That's because I didn't know what plumb-bobbing was, and I still don't understand it. Whenever I try to plumb-bob a putt, all I see is the non-conforming grip on my putter.

I have no idea what I shot on my first nine holes of golf. Three figures, but that's about as close as I can come. I did, however, lash a frozen rope over the third baseman's head on one of the holes. The ball wound up in a ditch. Ground rule double.

I got better at golf the more I played. I even had an eagle on the seventh hole at Brown Bell, the treacherous 180-yard par four. Yes, par four.

One of Mr. Brown's cows' favorite grazing spot was No. 7, which made the hole quite difficult. First, your shot might be going right at the hole and then hit a cow.

God knows where your shot might land after hitting a cow, and what if the cow died because your tee shot hit it in the head? You'd probably have to pay Mr. Brown for his dead cow, and it was such pre-swing thoughts that made the hole so fearsome.

There was also the matter of what cows inevitably will leave in the vicinity of where they have been grazing. Plumb-bob that.

But swinging at the ball and making putts through bovine calling cards was not the most difficult thing I encountered during my early days as a golfer. And neither was stepping in some, which was difficult to get off the tread of a tennis shoe, which is what I wore to play golf before noticing that real golfers wore spikes. After that, I played in my baseball spikes. When I stepped in the aforementioned substance wearing baseball shoes, it was easier to get the substance off since there was no smearing.

The most difficult thing about golf was that I had to locate every ball, no matter where it went or how long it took to find it. The term "lost ball" didn't mean loss of stroke and distance to me. It meant financial disaster. Losing a ball would mean I'd have to fork over another quarter for one of those slightly-used, mud-covered, oft-cut Club Specials. A quarter would buy a gallon of gasoline and a Dairy Queen hamburger in those days. A quarter, in other words, was a by-God quarter.

I searched through woods. I searched through briars that cut my hands and legs. I searched through muddy ditches, up under Mr. Brown's tractor, and, after a particularly nasty slice on the first tee, inside the hayloft in Mr. Brown's yard.

(At this point, some people inevitably will have thoughts regarding the rural sexual ritual known as rolling in the hay. As I mentioned earlier, nobody had sex in my hometown until after the Beatles came and Elvis got fat, so the term is not applicable in this case.

I should explain, however, there was a non-sexual activity that also went on in barns in those days. It was known as rat-killing. Here's how it worked:

A number of farmers, including my friend Mike Murphy's father, Mr. Red, kept their corn in their barns. Rats like corn. They especially like feeding on corn at night. Thus the modern term, "lounge rat."

The idea was to gather a group, all armed with .22 rifles. We would sneak into the barn at night and, at a given signal, a light would be thrown at the corn bin. The rats, quite surprised and temporarily blinded, would begin to run in circles in search of cover. The participants in the event would cut down on them with their .22s.

It was a joyous experience, probably like the one Indians had when they attacked a wagon train at night and massacred all the pioneers.

I realize none of this has anything to do with golf whatsoever, but when you throw a little sex and violence into a book, studies show sales usually rise as a result. I'm trying to raise enough money to buy a dozen Slazengers, which now run somewhere around what you once could buy a new Buick for.)

I was so diligent in my efforts to find any of my missing Club Specials that I played my entire first year of golf with the same three balls . . . which reminds me of what happened one day at Brown Bell.

I was in the clubhouse when a guy came in bleeding profusely from the head. I said, "What on earth happened to you?"

He said, "I was out on No. 7 with my wife and mother-in-law. My mother-in-law hit her ball in the woods and I was trying to help her find it. I came upon a cow and I noticed something protruding from under its tail. I looked closer and what was protruding was a golf ball.

"My mother-in-law was nearby, so I raised the cow's tail and pointed to the ball and asked, 'Does this look like yours?' and she beat me over the head with her seven-iron."

You and I know, of course, the preceding didn't occur in the clubhouse at Brown Bell but is actually an old joke. I know several hundred other old golf jokes, some of which will be included later in the book. Most of them — no, all of them — are better than the story about the guy and his mother-in-law, but you never serve the dessert first.

During my senior year in high school, I stepped up a notch in golf sophisticaton. I bought a used bag at Brown Bell, my mother gave me three new Maxflis for Christmas, and I discovered another golf course.

South of Moreland, in adjoining Troup County, was Hogansville, where most everybody worked in a rubber plant and the girls were supposed to be hot, but I never learned if that were true because the boys were supposed to be mad dogs in Hogansville and had no intention of allowing anybody from outside of town to mess with their women, a phrase people used in the sixties before women had double last names.

Hogansville also had a nine-hole golf course. There were no cows on the Hogansville course, but there were sand greens. (I'm not really sure "sand" greens is correct. You can say "grass" greens because grass is green. But sand isn't green. Or at least I've never seen any green sand. Sand is mostly white or brown. I suppose what would be more correct is to say Hogansville's golf course featured putting surfaces of sand.)

There are some advantages to putting surfaces made of sand. First, you never have to worry about a ball rolling off the putting surface. Balls tend to bury themselves when hit into sand. (The local rule was any time the ball hit on a sand green and disappeared under the sand, it was okay to take out a sand wedge and excavate in order to find it.)

Secondly, you didn't have to worry much about break while putting on a sand green. You simply made full turn with your putter and attempted to blast the ball straight into the hole.

The disadvantage involved in sand putting surfaces is after you walk all over them and dig large holes in them looking for your missing ball, they resemble what the beach probably looked like where they filmed all those Frankie Avalon-Annette Funicello movies.

So, after putting out on Hogansville's sand putting surfaces, it was necessary to locate the homemade dragging tool on each hole and smooth out the sand again, which took approximately ten minutes and was a large pain. Failure to drag the sand putting surface was considered the same breach of conduct as wearing purple patent-leather golf shoes at Augusta National while Clifford Roberts was still alive.

Hogansville, I am happy to report, eventually put in grass putting surfaces and expanded its course to eighteen holes. They also constructed a large building near the course and had professional wrestling matches there. One night an elderly woman watching the matches became so incensed at the antics of one of the bad guys that she walked over to the ring and, when he was pinned in a corner, she stuck her nail file into one of the poor man's legs. Hogansville was a tough town.

I continued to play golf after I entered college at the University of Georgia. It was at this point in my career that I discovered the agony involved when a golfer knows there is a great golf course in the area but he or she can't play on it because it's private.

The Athens Country Club course is a marvelous, plush Donald Ross layout. The Georgia golf team played there. The Southeastern Intercollegiate tournament was held there. Arnold Palmer played there when he was at Wake Forest.

I wanted to play there. But, no. I had to be content to play at area public courses, all a beat ahead of Brown Bell in Turin and sand greens, but a driver, three-wood, two-iron and wedge away from Athens Country Club.

What made things worse was as I drove to a public course in nearby Commerce, Georgia, I had to drive past the Athens Country Club. I could see the beautiful, par-four eighteenth and longed for the opportunity to play it. I felt like a hungry man passing Maxim's in Paris on his way to a soup line.

The golf course in Commerce did have some features in common with Brown Bell. It basically was a large pasture, too. The cows, however, were fenced off from the course and one didn't worry about stepping in and putting through what we discussed earlier.

There was the unique problem of Slim, the guy who drove the mower, however. When Slim decided to mow, he mowed. He didn't care if there was a group playing the hole he had decided to mow.

It often was a bit unnerving to be standing over an approach shot, knowing Slim was behind you in the mower. I don't know if Slim ever mowed down a golfer, but the possibility was always in your mind.

What Slim did one day, however, was run over my ball with his mower. I was in a foursome and had hit a marvelous tee shot on a par four.

Before I could get to my ball, however, Slim ran over it and cut it into many pieces.

"What should I do?" I asked one of my opponents.

"Find the biggest piece and hit it," he answered.

I must point out that I did finally get to play the Athens Country Club course. A fiendish friend came up with the idea.

"Look," he said, "there's no starter at the first tee. All we have to do is hide in the bushes near the swimming pool. When there's nobody about to tee off, we simply run out there and hit. When we finish eighteen, we can slip behind the trees near the tennis courts and then run to our car."

"I have just one question," I said.

"What's that?" replied my devious friend.

"Do you think it will be safe to hit a mulligan on the first tee?"

I'm not certain how many times we did sneak on the country club course at Athens, but it was well into double figures by the time we finally got caught.

The club pro happened to be riding around the course one day and saw two young men he didn't recognize walking and carrying their own bags.

"Are you boys guests of a member?" he asked us as we were set to tee off on the par five, sixteenth.

He had us. We knew he had us and he knew he had us, but we did try to talk our way out of a terribly embarrassing situation.

"I'm a landscape architect major," I said, and I was assigned to play the course and do a report. "Didn't my professor phone?"

"No professor called," said the pro.

My friend then gave it a shot.

"I'm leaving town tomorrow to join the Army and go to Viet Nam to fight for our country against the fearsome possibility of communism spreading further into the free world. Since I was a small boy, being raised by my poor grandparents after my mom and dad died in a tenement fire, I have always wanted to play this golf course. And since I might not be coming back from war (he choked a little here to signify he was fighting back tears), I decided to slip onto your wonderful golf course. If you love your country," he continued, "you will allow us to finish this round and not press charges against us."

The pro said, "If I ever catch you little turds out here again, I'm calling the police. You have five minutes to be off the property." The man clearly wasn't a patriot.

I continued to play golf after college. I had reached the point where I could actually break ninety on occasion. I had not reached the point, however, where I had enough money to join a private club.

I moved to Atlanta, home of such wonderful, historic tracts as East Lake Country Club, where Bob Jones's locker is still preserved, Peachtree Golf Club, which Jones designed, the grand old Capital City Club course and the new Atlanta Country Club course, home of a new stop on the pro tour.

I never got near those courses, however. I played public courses where the greens often looked like the landscape of the moon, which we actually would see on television in a short period of time.

What caused me to give up golf a few years later was a duck hook. A duck hook is when you hit the ball, it goes out about one hundred yards, then takes a ninety-degree turn to the left into either a lake, the woods, the course maintenance shack, the foursome on the adjoining fairway, or, as my duck hook became even worse, into the adjoining county.

I'm not certain why a duck hook is called that, but when you hit one, your playing partners usually respond by quacking. There is nothing quite so demeaning as hooking a ball into Never Never Land (you'll never make another par as long as you live hitting the ball like that) and having your playing partners begin quacking in unison.

I tried everything to get rid of my duck hook. I teed the ball lower, then I teed it higher. I moved the ball up in my stance; I moved it back. I aimed right. I even thought of having my right hand amputated when somebody said to me, "You're getting too much right hand into your swing. That's why you're hooking the ball."

What I did was quit. One day, I finished a round and had picked up on practically every hole, had lost a dozen golf balls and had set a new world record for swearing.

I said, "This is a stupid game in the first place, and it really isn't a sport because you can smoke while you play it, and God doesn't want me to play it or He would have answered my prayers by now and I wouldn't still have this [an impressive litany of filthy modifiers] duck hook."

I took up tennis. As a matter of fact, I became obsessed with tennis. I played tennis every day for the next sixteen years. When it was cold or raining, I played in an indoor facility I was able to join for a few bucks, not the thousands country clubs wanted. I became a fair tennis player. My doubles partner and I were even once ranked thirteenth in the state in the thirty-five-year-old doubles. He was No. 2 in the South with another guy, but I don't care.

I used to laugh at golfers after I became a tennis player. "Golf's not a sport," I said. "The ball sits still while you try to hit. Try to return a topspin forehand, if you think golf is tough."

Golfers don't get any exercise. It takes all day to play. I never lost a single tennis ball in my sixteen years as a player. My language improved as a tennis player. If I hit a bad shot in tennis, it wasn't fifteen seconds until I was in another point and had completely forgotten about the bad shot. I would brood for days over a missed putt when I played golf.

The change didn't come on suddenly. It came on over a period of years. God didn't intend for people to play tennis every day for sixteen years, either. That's because the longer you play tennis, the more your body tells you it's a sport that can create invalids.

I developed tennis elbow. That's where your elbow always feels like there's a little man with a pitchfork inside it. I developed tennis toe. That's where your big toes swell to twice their regular size. I developed tennis shins. That's from bouncing around on hard tennis courts for years.

The bottoms of my feet turned into two giant callouses that often cracked and bled.

I got bursitis in my right shoulder. I began taking four aspirin a set for the pain.

And one morning in 1984, I awakened and was so crippled I could no longer brush my teeth with my right arm.

So I tried brushing my teeth with my left arm. Impossible. If I didn't stop playing tennis, I reasoned, all my teeth would fall out in a matter of months and I would be in a wheelchair.

Yes, I did seek medical advice. My doctor advised me, "Stop playing tennis."

So I did. And then I took up golf again at the age of thirty-eight, because I certainly couldn't play baseball anymore, I had no interest in getting into automobile racing, bowling is for nerds and you have to wear those ugly shoes and the ball is too heavy, and riding a bicycle all over town in those tight pants seemed to me a sport people who were in the science club in high school would enjoy.

And by this time, I had become financially successful to the point that I could afford the latest golf equipment and I could afford to join a private club.

I ordered a set of Pings (blue dot), bought one of those big Jack Nicklaus putters (which you could kill a rat with), a pair of white Foot-joys, and a golf bag with seven compartments. I also bought a membership in the Ansley Golf Club (founded in 1912) in Atlanta.

This time it was going to be different. I bought some golf shirts and sweaters with the name of my club on them. I bought some of those cute little half-socks like golfers wear, and I decided before I went out to play, I would take my first golf lesson to learn once and for all the proper way to strike a golf ball so as to keep it out of places it had no business going into. If I still had my duck hook, I was certain my PGA golf professional could teach me a way to rid myself of it forever.

We went down to the range, me and my pro. Here's what he told me:

"Put forty percent of your weight on your left foot, sixty percent on your right. Bend your knees slightly, but not too slightly, and do a semi-squat, but not too semi.

"Relax your arms and hands. Pretend you are shaking hands with a lady, say your grandmother. Don't pretend you are shaking hands with a female lawyer because if you don't squeeze her hand in the same manner you would shake hands with one of your male friends, she will become offended and knee you in the groin.

"It is very difficult to swing a golf club after being kneed in the groin.

"Okay. Now, take the club back slowly along the ground after your groin has stopped hurting. Turn your hips and shoulders and lift your left foot, shifting all your weight to your right.

"Bring the club up parallel and hinge your left wrist. Take a deep breath and think about bringing the club down on an inside-out plane. Now, plant your left foot back on the ground and bring the club back down towards the ball. Do not *hit* at the ball. Swing through the ball.

"And I forgot the part about keeping your right arm close to your body and your left arm straight on the takeaway. And did I mention the club dress code? Something else to think about as you bring the club back towards the ball is, 'Do my long shorts have at least a sixteen-inch inseam?'

"Now, begin to shift your weight back towards your left side. Make certain to keep your head down and behind the ball at impact.

"At impact, never ask yourself, 'Where is this ball going to go? Will it go into the water? Out of bounds? Backwards? Into the clubhouse and strike my assistant, who is selling a golf shirt for eighty dollars, on the head, causing him permanent brain damage? And where is that female lawyer who kneed me in the groin? I wonder what she will charge to represent me in the subsequent lawsuit?'

"If you start asking yourself these questions, you will tighten up and not swing through the ball and you might lose all your money, your house, your family and your friends.

"Finish your swing with the upper half of your body facing the target, and all the weight on your left side. Did I mention pronation? That was back in the thirties when alcohol consumption was made illegal in the United States.

"You may be asking yourself, at some point during your back swing, 'What in the hell does that have to do with golf?'

"Well, how would you like to go out and shoot 108 and not be able to get a drink in the men's grill?

"Just remember the golf swing is very simple, and I'd like to see you swing at one, but a new shipment of eight hundred dollar sweaters is due in the pro shop at any minute, and I'll have to be there to sign for them. The Brinks people are very touchy about that."

So I've been playing golf again now for six years. I've played golf in such exotic places as Hawaii, California, Mexico, Ireland, Scotland and Alabama.

I am as obsessed by golf as I was obsessed by tennis. But my right shoulder hurts only when it rains now, the bleeding callouses are gone from the bottom of my feet, my tennis elbow and shins and toes have all gone away. I do have golf hands now, however.

I play so much golf my right hand is richly tanned. My left hand, where my golf glove goes, is the color of sheetrock. Small children see me off the golf course and ask their mothers, "Mommy, what's wrong with that man's hands?"

I don't duck hook anymore. As a matter of fact, lately I've been orangutan fading the ball. But my game is coming along. I started out with a twenty-two handicap. I have it down to an eleven, which is as low as I ever want to go, because if I get into the single digits, I won't get any shots anymore, I'll be upset if I don't break eighty every time out, and I'll have to buy a bag with my name on it, which is against the Rules of Golf if you don't have a single-digit handicap.

What this book proposes to do is to talk about golf as it has never been talked about before. This book will not improve your golf game. But I hope there are a few yuks along the way.

Just remember while you are reading this book, to keep your head down. Reading is a lot easier that way. But if you can't, after all these years of looking up to see what mischief your golf ball has gotten into as a result of your hitting it, nail the book to the ceiling.

By the way, I stole the title for this book. I saw it printed on a T-shirt in the golf shop at Busch Gardens in Williamsburg, Virginia. If you are a beginning golfer, no, you can't wear a T-shirt when you play golf. If you can't live with that, go bowling. Hey, nice shoes.

The fundamentalist preacher was quick to admonish his congregation for violating the Sabbath, but being an ardent golfer, he himself was often tempted to play golf on sunny Sundays. One spring Sunday morning dawned so glorious that he could not resist the temptation. He sneaked out to the course before anyone else and teed off.

When he was on the third tee, facing a 440-yard par four with a dogleg left, an angel spotted him and reported the transgression to God. "We must punish this sinner, Lord," said the angel.

"I shall," said the Lord.

The preacher hit his drive long and straight, but then a miraculous thing happened: the ball hooked slightly, gained momentum and carried all the way to the green. It hit softly on the front edge, hopped twice, and rolled gently into the cup for an ace.

The angel turned to God and said, "I thought you intended to punish him. But, instead, you just allowed him to hit the shot of a lifetime."

"Oh, but I did punish him," said God. "Who's he going to tell?"

Snickers For Your Knickers

There's an old story about two fellows watching an unattractive woman cross the street.

"Lord, Cordie Mae Poovey is uglier than a train wreck," says one.

"Don't be so rough on her," says the other. "She can't help being ugly."

"Maybe not," says the first, "but at least she could've stayed home."

***

Within that story, allowing a good bit of room for artistic interpretation, is my philosophy about golf course attire.

The last statistic I saw said that fewer than ten percent of the people who play golf in America can break ninety and that the average score is well over a hundred. That means that nine out of ten of you are never going to be called "good golfers." In fact, it's more likely that your game will be called "possum ugly." But just because you play ugly doesn't mean you have to look ugly. If you do, you might as well stay home.

The truth of the matter is that it's downright hard to look bad on a golf course. Where else, besides New York City and Southern California, can you wear a purple plaid shirt with chartreuse pants and not turn a head?

On a golf course you can dress like a clown and have people ask you where you shop. You can wear baby blue shoes and not even get propositioned. You can wear Bermuda shorts with white socks and still use the men's restroom.

Even polyester, the fabric of choice among used car salesmen and house painters, is haute couture on the golf course. It is used to make, among other things, lime green pants without belt loops, the kind usually worn by insurance salesmen who shop in the portly section of men's stores. Those same pants, in smaller sizes, can be quite fashionable on the links.

Polyester is lightweight and stretches with the wearer, making it an ideal fabric for athletics. It has only three natural enemies – Ralph Lauren, the Junior League and fire.

Some golf courses have become designated non-smoking areas, not because of the cancer risk but because of the fire risk. Polyester is so flammable that a stray ash from a cigarette could ignite you, and the resulting smoke and noxious fumes could leave your playing partners coughing for several holes. It is also not good golf etiquette to barbecue on the course.

Proper golf wear is generally either very cheap or outrageously expensive. K mart has some of the best deals at very low prices. These stunning outfits usually can be found in the sections marked "Dress for Success" or "The Junior Executive." (WARNING: Do not wear these clothes anywhere except on the golf course, unless, of course, you are a used car salesman or house painter.)

If there's not a K mart nearby or if your social standing in the community does not allow you to shop there, then the only place you're likely to find such colorful clothes is in golf pro shops.

Pro shops are like exclusive boutiques – there's usually no one to wait on you, the selections are small, and the prices are outrageous. They take your basic fifteen-dollar polyester and cotton knit shirt, have the name of your club (or somebody else's club) embroidered on the pocket, put it in a plastic bag and charge you forty-five dollars for it.

If you dare to complain about the price or, Heaven forbid, try to haggle the price down, you are treated like Jethro Bodine with herpes. What you see in their eyes but is never spoken is, "If you can afford to be a member of this club, you can afford to pay forty-five dollars for a shirt."

That's precisely why you cannot afford to pay forty-five dollars for the shirt: your club dues are only slightly less than your house payment.

In the pro shop of an exclusive private club, I recently encountered a new high-water (or low intelligence) level: eighty dollars for a knit golf shirt. It didn't even have the name of the club on the pocket, just a little golfer embroidered on the inside of the collar.

"Why on earth does this shirt cost eighty dollars instead of the usual forty-five?" I asked the pro, who acted like I'd just passed gas.

"Because, sir, that embroidered image of Bobby Jones on the collar makes it most exclusive and worth every penny of the price in sheer prestige," he said.

"Bobby Jones?" I said. "I could have sworn that was Orville Moody."

"Certainly not, sir. The Orville Moody version sells for $19.95, but you wouldn't want to be caught dead in it on a private course."

There are, in fact, certain things you wouldn't want to be caught dead in on any respectable golf course, public or private. Following are some of the classic no-nos from *GRIZZARD'S GUIDELINES FOR PROPER GOLF COURSE ATTIRE:*

- Do not wear tennis, basketball or running shoes on the golf course. They make courts, gyms and roads for those. I used to play golf with a man who was a stickler for proper dress and etiquette. "If I owned a golf course," he often said, "I'd have me a trap door right in front of the cash register. When some fool came up wearing tennis shoes and said he wanted to play golf, I'd just pull the switch on the trap door and send him back where he came from." Like I said, the man was a stickler.

- Do not wear golf shoes with little flaps over the laces. Only Yankees and tourists (south of Washington, D.C., they're one and the same) wear those. Likewise, do not wear golf shoes with little loops on the sides for holding tees. Only female Yankees and female tourists wear those.

• Speaking of Yankees and tourists, do not wear dark stretch socks pulled up to the knee with baggy Bermuda shorts. If you wear Bermuda shorts, they should fall approximately three inches above the knee. Save the coaching shorts, running shorts and old bathing suits for the company picnic. Tube socks and tennis socks with fuzzy balls at the heels also are not appropriate for the golf course (or anywhere else, for that matter). Rule No. 214, subsection E, of the USGA Rules of Golf also prohibits the presence of fuzzy dice anywhere on any golf course. (They are, however, required for play on any Mexican course.)

• Do not wear any hat that has fishing lures or advertising for farm machinery or chewing tobacco on it. Also do not wear any hat that has a ♥ on it, as in, "I ♥ my dog . . . and my wife." Also, do not wear hats with supposedly cute sayings, even if the cute saying is, "Save the South. Buy a Yankee a Bus Ticket."

Even proper golf hats can be dangerous. Once I was having a late lunch with a friend after a round of golf. He was wearing a hat with the word PING across the front (it came with his new Ping clubs). A good old boy walked in, spotted the hat, and yelled across the restaurant, "Hey, Ping, whar's Pong?"

• Beware of any golfer whose hat, shirt, pants, socks, shoes and tees are all the same color. If that color happens to be pink, do *not* help him look for his ball in the woods, and be alert whenever you mark your ball.

As a final word on proper golf attire, I must address the issue of knickers – the traditional golf pants that end just below the knees. Knickers look pretty good on Gene Sarazen and Payne Stewart, but most of us look like Mickey Rooney, or Andy, in them.

It is my personal opinion, based on extensive research and on being easily embarrassed, that only golfers with a handicap of ten or less should ever wear knickers, and even then only on private courses. Knickers on a public course will get you cut.

In Search Of The Larger Sweet Spot

It used to be that when a man or woman went into a store to buy golf clubs, the only question they were asked was, "Right-handed or left-handed?"

Nowadays that answer won't even get you to the cash register, much less to the first tee.

I went shopping for new clubs recently, and here's how it went:

"Hi, I'm interested in buying a new set of golf clubs."

"Fine, sir, just have a seat while we fill out this information sheet. Now, I need to know your height, weight, shoe size, any distingushing birthmarks or scars, frequency of bowel movement, current handicap – other than your looks, and your annual income."

"Hey, I just wanted to buy some golf clubs, not apply for a secret service job."

"Sir, ours is a very scientific business, based on years of research and development for the sole purpose of improving your golf game. But if you don't appreciate all the trouble and expense we've gone to just for you, then I'll have to ask you to leave right now."

"Do you know my ex-wife?"

"No, sir, I'm just here to do my job, thankless as it is. Now, are you interested in wooden woods or metal woods?"

"Isn't *metal wood* an oxymoron?"

"Sir, I'm an expert in golf equipment, not in animal husbandry. I have no idea why your ox isn't smart. Now, if you want real wood woods, we have this set crafted from genuine, aged, hand-selected, U.S. grade-A persimmon."

"Sounds like a beef commercial to me."

"Sir, for the second time, I'm not into animals. Now, if you prefer metal woods, we have this new model which features a lightweight steel shaft with a graphite and kevlar compound interwoven and baked onto the butt of the club."

"The Jim Bakker model?"

"Excuse me, sir?"

"Never mind."

"This particular club also comes in jumbo size that is forty percent larger than a conventional driver. The larger size provides a bigger sweet spot that is far more forgiving."

"If only I could find a woman like that."

"It comes standard with a ten-degree loft, and we also have it in a graphite head reinforced with boron."

"Isn't graphite what they use in pencils? Will I have to sharpen my driver occasionally? And when did Twenty-Mule Team Boron quit making detergent and go into the golf business?"

"Sir, once and for all, I don't know what your fetish is with oxen, cattle and mules, but I wish you would leave me out of it. If it's kicks you're after, I suggest this ceramic-headed driver."

"Ceramic, like in toilet bowls?"

"Yes sir. The manufacturer recommends that you spray it with Lysol after each round. For a man of your tastes, I also could recommend this state-of-the-art, electric-powered driver made of high-tech thermoplastic that was originally developed for the bulletproof vest industry. It comes with a one-thousand-foot retractable extension cord that stores in the heel of the driver. For a few dollars more, it can be converted for battery operation."

"Tell me about the irons. Are they still metal, or do you also offer wooden irons these days?"

"They're metal, sir, but you can get them cast or forged with a black-face, the Al Jolson model, or a beryllium copper finish. They're all perimeter weighted, and the lower clubs have wider flange soles to encourage skimming."

"Skimming? I've got a banker friend serving five years for that. And I've done all the perimeter waiting I care to do; the traffic was awful on the way over here. Look, this is a lot more complicated than I ever dreamed. Why don't I just buy a dozen balls and come back some other time?"

"Fine, sir, if that's your wish. What dimple pattern do you prefer?"

"I've had it with these personal questions. I'm out of here."

"But wait a moment, sir. We haven't even discussed your putter yet."

All of this new, high-tech equipment is more than I can comprehend. But there are several things I know for sure about golf equipment:

• Whether you play ninety- or one hundred-compression balls, whether you play white, yellow, red or orange balls, they're all hard to hit under six inches of water.

• The new oversized putters are really old traditional Bullseye putters with thyroid conditions.

• The metal woods that are so chic today weren't nearly so cool when they were standard equipment at driving ranges twenty years ago.

• No matter how good the equipment is, you've still got to put the club face squarely on the ball for it to work.

• By the time a man can afford to lose a golf ball, he can't hit it that far.

And I Thought A Swing Plane Was An Orgy At 30,000 Feet

The golf pro is giving a lesson to one of his club members. "Now, first of all, just take a few swings without hitting the ball," says the pro.

"Hell, I've already mastered that shot," says the pupil. "I'm paying you to teach me how to hit it."

***

Okay, you want to learn to play golf. Or, if you already play, you want to learn to play better. Everybody does. To my knowledge, no one in the world is ever pleased with his golf game, or even with a single round.

If you shoot ninety-one, you spend the next three hours talking about the two three-foot putts you missed that would have put you in the eighties. And if you shoot seventy, you bore the fuzz off a peach talking about the six-foot putt you missed that would have put you in the sixties. Either way, whether you're a scruff or a scratch golfer, you're never satisfied with your score.

So how do you improve your game and get rid of that extra shot or two?

You can subscribe to golf magazines and read the tips, but that's as dangerous as reading – and heeding – your horoscope. You can always spot these guys on the golf course. They're the ones who count aloud while they're swinging.

You can rent an instructional video, but you don't find many televisions on practice tees, and every swing is beautiful in your den. Besides, I suspect Kim Basinger is the only person in the world who could make indoor golf seem like fun. I don't know how she would do it, but after watching her in the movie *9 1/2 Weeks*, I'm confident she would come up with something. My palms sweat just imagining what she could do in the front seat of a golf cart.

After that, there is only one alternative left, and this is to take a lesson from a certified, genuine, sanctioned PGA Club Professional, His Honor, Sir. He is the handsome, well-dressed, tanned person who hustles eighty-dollar golf shirts and slips off occasionally to have sex with the wife of one of the members who just teed off and won't be home for five hours.

After taking about half a million dollars' worth of lessons from at least four hundred pros (I'm not married, so I don't worry about any of them slipping off to have sex with my wife. I do live with two black Labs, but let's not get into anything like that.), I have become convinced of a conspiracy.

Here's the deal: God picks out people and gives them Golf's Secret. These are the people who actually can shoot par or better. I'm not certain by what process God chooses these individuals.

Perhaps he does it at random. He's sitting there, dictating who will get what when they are born, and he says, "Okay, Hotchkiss gets a lot of hair, Windom gets great teeth, Matthews gets no zits when he's in high school, give Shirley Patton blue eyes and a rich daddy, and give Schwarz The Secret of Golf."

So, at any time on earth, there are maybe 10,000 people God has given The Secret of Golf.

The problem for the rest of us (I got quick hands and was born in the South) is that those who know The Secret of Golf have a pact not to tell the rest of us what it is because if everybody knew The Secret of Golf, pros who know the secret couldn't make any money giving lessons because we wouldn't need any.

So, when you take a golf lesson from a pro, consider that and the fact that nothing he says or shows you will actually work.

I will give you some examples:

- Your pro will talk a lot about the "proper swing plane." You are supposed to take the club away from the ball and bring it back in a perfect inside-out path every time you swing.

This is impossible, however, because when you take the club away from the ball, you can't see it anymore, so how are you going to bring it back on the proper swing plane when you can't see the damn thing?

- Your pro will talk about your alignment. He wants you to point your arms, hands, feet, shoulders, hips, eyes, nose, ears and pancreas in certain positions.

To do all this like he says to do it, you would need to be a contortionist, plus when you stoop over like he says to, it hurts your back and this guy is twenty-eight years old and his back hasn't started hurting yet. When your pro begins to talk about the proper alignment, take a pack of Doan's Pills out of your bag and eat four of them. They won't help your golf swing, but they will allow you to get out of the bed the next morning after our pro has made you try things with your body that are impossible after age thirty-five.

• Your pro will talk to you about weight transfer. When you take the club back, your weight should be on your right foot. As you bring the club toward the ball, you are supposed to shift your weight to your left foot. The same thing is required of you when you do the samba, the beguine and the Teaneck, New Jersey Hustle, and who does this person think you are? Fred Damn Astaire?

• Your pro will further confuse you by talking about your grip, your shoulder turn, your one-piece takeaway, your club release, the fact your head should become an immovable object and the fact your wife looks so lovely when the sun hits her hair in that special way while she's at the club pool wearing nothing but a cork and two Band-Aids.

He will use such words as "perpendicular," "horizontal" and "parallel." He will mention the rotation of the earth, gravity, the summer equinox, the equator and Norfolk, Virginia.

He will also mention that you need a complete new set of clubs and better-looking pair of golf shoes.

When your lesson is over, he will charge you forty dollars, make another couple hundred off your new clubs and shoes, and then call a friend who also knows The Secret and laugh at you for being a sucker.

So, the bad news is if you didn't come into the world with The Secret, you're not going to find it out and you'll be a hacker like the rest of us during your entire golfing life.

The only thing you can do is buy this book and read *GRIZZARD'S INSTRUCTIONS FOR GOLFERS WHO GOD LEFT OUT:*

- Keep you head down when you swing. This is made easier by pretending you are bobbing for apples. Except don't think what diseases you could get poking your nose and mouth into a bucket of water everybody else at the party has had their noses and mouth in.

- Watch the ball. Watch it go left, watch it go right, watch it go three inches, watch it land behind a tree, watch it go into the street and hit a new Saab, watch it sky, shank, dribble off the tee, hit a low-flying aircraft or your pro who is giving another sucker a lesson over at the practice range.

On second thought, don't watch the ball. Too many horrible, ungodly, unmentionable things can happen to it.

- Hold your club with a death grip. You don't want to further embarrass yourself by having the club come loose from your hands and killing a member of your foursome. Then again, if the son of a bitch wouldn't concede a two-foot putt to you on the last hole, he deserves to die.

• Swing as hard as you can. Golf is an expensive game and you want to get your money's worth.

• Swing as fast as you can. The sooner you finish, the sooner you can get to the bar in the men's grill.

• Finish high: When you go into the bar in the men's grill, drink as many drinks as you had triple bogeys. This will allow you to end your day not giving a damn how many triple bogeys you had. But don't attempt to drive home. Make the pro drive you in his new $90,000 two-seater Mercedes convertible with the power roof you helped him buy.

One other note: When all else fails, consider these inspiring words from Dan Quayle, "A wasted mind is a terrible thing to bogey."

"I just got a new set of golf clubs for my husband."

"Gee, what a great trade!"

Rules Are Bent To Be Broken

Golf can be a humiliating, bumbling, frustrating game, especially if you have to play by the rules. And there are a million of 'em – rules covering everything from how many clubs you can carry to when you can touch your ball.

Worse than that, golfers have to call penalties on themselves. Almost every other sport has umpires and referees to be the bad guys (that's why they all wear black uniforms), but golfers are on the honor system.

Say in basketball you're under the basket and notice that the referee is screened out, so you take your elbow and bury it in the ribcage of the defender who has been frisking you all night long. The guy with the collapsed lung rolls on the floor like he's having a grand mal seizure, while you seize the moment to score an easy basket. You have broken the rules (and maybe a couple of ribs) but didn't get caught. It's a good feeling and your teammates congratulate you.

Now say you're on the golf course and hit your drive into the woods. When you finally find your ball, it's sitting down in a hole directly behind a tree with more branches than the Chase Manhattan Bank. If, however, the ball were two feet further to the right, you would have a clear shot to the green with an unobstructed swing. If the stupid groundskeeper hadn't watered the fairway last night, the ball would have rolled those two extra feet . . . after it ricocheted off the rake in the fairway bunker and scooted through the rough and into the woods.

You have obviously been victimized by cruel fate, so you seek retribution in the only way you know how – by moving your ball two feet to the right when your opponents are not looking. You hit a great second shot, make the birdie putt and go on to win the match one-up. Like the basketball player, you have broken the rules and didn't get caught. But rather than feeling good about it, you feel like a flattened skunk who's been dead on the road for four days.

So who decided to pick on golfers? The game was already difficult enough to make grown men wear skirts, so why make it harder with a bunch of nitpicking rules? I figure the wee Scotsman who first made up all those rules must have been wearing his kilt too high or his pouch too low. Or both.

Being the great humanitarian that I am, I have devised a kinder, gentler set of rules for golf. The next time you're out for a round, use these modified rules and see if you don't shave several strokes off your score and leave the course feeling much better about yourself . . . and mankind.

THE MILLIGAN RULE

Most golfers know what a "mulligan" is. That's when you hit a second shot off the first tee because your first shot went into the rose bed of the little old lady who lives across the street from the first fairway. The "milligan rule" takes that logic a step further. If you don't like your first shot on *any* tee, hit another one (that's your "milligan"). If that shot is lousy, too, hit a third shot, called a "McMilligan." If you *still* don't have a good shot, drive the cart out into the middle of the fairway about 250 yards from the tee and drop your ball there. That's called a "Grover McMilligan," named for the famous card cheat who died in a lynching accident in 1926.

MOVING THE BALL IN THE ROUGH

Under my modified rules of golf, you may not only move your ball in the rough, you may ignore the rough altogether and place your ball back in the fairway – ten yards closer to the hole for each form of reptilia spotted while you were over there in the weeds looking for your ball.

SAND RULE

Whose idea was it to put sand on a golf course in the first place? If I'd wanted to play in the sand, I'd have gone to the beach. When your ball goes into the sand, remove it as quickly as possible and place it on a nice flat spot on the green (no closer to the pin, however, than the length of a standard beach umbrella).

LOST BALL RULE

Let's say you hit your ball into the water and it can't be retrieved. What you do is subtract two strokes from your eventual score on that hole. You deserve it. After all, you just paid nearly three bucks for a brand-new golf ball that is now a toy for a fish.

TREE RULE

If you are aiming at a tree and hit it, you must play your ball as it lies. If, however, you are aiming down the middle of the fairway and your ball hits a tree, advance the ball fifty yards toward the green for each variety of pine tree you can name.

TWO-PUTT RULE

If your ball still isn't in the hole after two putts, pick it up and place it in the hole. Be careful not to touch the edge of the cup, which is a one-shot penalty. Rules are rules. If your opponent complains, pick him up and place his head in the hole.

BEER RULE

At the end of your round, count up the number of beers you drank during the round and subtract that number from your total score. If you had been sober, that's probably what you would have shot in the first place. (NOTE: Your net score must be a positive number; that is, you may not drink more beers than you had strokes during the round. Actually, you *may* drink more than that, but you can't deduct them from your score. In such cases, a bronze statue of you will be erected outside the men's grill.)

TWO-CLUB LENGTH RULE

Many times when a golfer hits a shot where he's not supposed to, such as under the concession stand, he is given relief and allowed to move his ball two club lengths in any direction no closer to the hole.

I think that is an excellent rule, but unfortunately it has been misinterpreted for years. Under my modified rules, the two clubs in question should be your home golf club and your favorite nightspot.

My home golf course, for instance, is approximately two miles from my favorite watering hole, Harvey's Dance and Ratchet Club, where they work on your car while you drink and dance. Therefore, I can move my ball up to two miles in any direction no closer to the hole.

SNAKE RULE

This one deserves an extended explanation. After all, snakes rank right up there with lightning, flying in bad weather at night, dentists and revenge-minded ex-wives as the things I fear most in this life.

One day not long ago I was playing golf at the beautiful Melrose course on Daufuskie Island, South Carolina. On the par four fourteenth hole, I hooked my drive into the woods. As I drove off in my cart in search of it, my playing partner said, "Be careful. They've been seeing a lot of snakes lately."

"What kind of snakes have they been seeing?" I asked.

"Rattlesnakes, I guess," he said.

I don't know why I asked such a silly question. As far as I'm concerned a snake is a snake. I didn't pay attention enough in Boy Scouts to be able to determine when I step on a snake whether it is going to bite me, coil around me and squeeze me to death or talk about all the rats it has been eating lately.

"If they ain't got shoulders," my boyhood friend and idol, Weyman C. Wannamaker, Jr., a great American, used to say, "I don't want to be near them."

Weyman's uncle had frightened him with stories about the dreaded "cottonmouth water rattler."

"My uncle says that's the meanest snake there is," Weyman explained. "They'll follow you home and wait for you to come out of the house the next morning."

"Do you think it's safe to go into the woods after my ball?" I asked my partner, as I reminded myself that this temporarily lost golf ball only cost $2.50.

"Just be careful around thick brush and fallen logs," he said.

I drove my cart into the woods and was about to get out when I noticed that all I could see around me was thick brush and fallen logs.

"One other thing," my partner yelled to me. "Snakes climb up trees, and sometimes they can fall off on your head."

I might have been able to deal with thick brush and the fallen logs. The part about a snake falling on my head did it, however. I declared my ball lost, took the necessary penalty, and from that point on played by the "snake rule," which clearly states, "Any player who hits a ball anywhere there might be a snake can forget about that ball and drop another in the fairway with no penalty."

I was at Melrose for four more wonderful days and, after inventing the snake rule, remained out of the woods and never saw snake one.

My partner, meanwhile, had to play golf with his wife one day.

"She went into the woods on No. 11 and saw a snake," he explained. "Best thing that ever happened to me."

"What do you mean by that?" I asked.

"The minute she stopped running," he said, "she gave up golf . . . forever."

***

My modified rules of golf have proven so successful for Americans that I felt, in the spirit of international cooperation (and in exchange for a free weekend at a golf resort, which required that I write about it), I should extend my efforts to cover Mexican golf.

My research was conducted at the luxurious Club Med in Ixtapa, Mexico, where the quality of the facility is rivaled only by the dedication of the efficient, trained staff which services the 135 rooms, each with its own telephone and cable television, and the restaurant uses only the freshest ingredients, regardless of how old they are. With that out of the way, here follows *GRIZZARD'S LIBERTARIAN RULES FOR MEXICAN GOLF:*

THE BURRO RULE

If a burro hee-haws during your backswing, you get an automatic par on the hole as retribution for your interruption. If your ball lands on what burros occasionally leave on Mexican golf courses, get your caddy to remove the ball and wash it thoroughly, give yourself a birdie and give your caddy an extra five hundred pesos for his trouble.

THE CROCODILE RULE

There are lots of crocodiles on Mexican golf courses. If you hit your ball into the water, make your caddy swim out and find it. If he is eaten by a crocodile, subtract ten strokes from your score for having wasted five hundred pesos.

THE RALPH NADER UNSAFE-AT-ANY-SPEED RULE

There are no brakes on Mexican golf carts. Hit two balls off the tee of any hole where you have to drive the cart down a steep embankment. If you are not maimed or killed in the cart, you may pick the best of your two tee shots.

THE NIGHT OF THE IGUANA RULE

There are lots of iguanas – large, ugly lizards – on Mexican golf courses. If you see one, divide Roseanne Barr's weight by four and subtract the total from your score. If you don't know Roseanne Barr's weight, put three caddies and a golf cart on a scale and use that total.

THE TEQUILA RULE

Take the number of tequila shots you had the night

before, add the number of times you got into a fight as a result of drinking all that tequila and then go back to bed. Nobody could play golf in your condition.

THE MONTEZUMA'S REVENGE RULE

If you have ignored everybody's advice and drank the water in Mexico anyway, hit your ball into the woods every chance you get. You will need to.

THE PEPTO BISMOL RULE

Better to be eaten by a crocodile in a water hazard than to be in Mexico without it.

Clifton was having a beer in the men's grill when Tony came in. "Hey, did you hear the terrible news about Newton?" asked Tony.

"No, what happened?"

"He finished his round early Saturday, went home and caught his wife in bed with another man. Shot 'em both deader than a doornail."

"Well," said Clifton, "it could have been worse."

"Worse? How?"

"If he'd come home early on Friday, he'd have shot me."

After an enjoyable eighteen holes of golf, a man stopped in a bar for a beer before heading home. There he struck up a conversation with a ravishing young beauty. They had a couple of drinks, liked each other, and soon she invited him over to her apartment. For two hours they made mad, passionate love.

On the way home, the man's conscience started bothering him something awful. He loved his wife and didn't want this unplanned indiscretion to ruin their relationship, so he decided the only thing to do was come clean.

"Honey," he said when he got home, "I have a confession to make. After I played golf today, I stopped by the bar for a beer, met a beautiful woman, went back to her apartment and made love to her for two hours. I'm sorry, it won't ever happen again, and I hope you'll forgive me."

His wife scowled at him and said, "Don't lie to me, you sorry scumbag! You played thirty-six holes, didn't you?"

Polies, Whammies, Pukies, Bonkers & Lloyd Bridges

A rotund golfer was arguing for more shots when the bet was being made. "You guys have a tremendous advantage over me because I have to putt from memory."

"From memory? What are you talking about?" asked his opponent.

"It's sad but simple," he explained, patting his belly. "When I put the ball where I can see it, I can't reach it; when I put it where I can reach it, I can't see it."

***

I'm not certain just how many people would play golf if they couldn't gamble. You don't have to gamble when you play golf, of course, but who wants to roll in a long birdie putt and not make somebody have to pay for it?

The problem in golf gambling, however, is that most golfers are also liars, especially when it comes to their handicaps.

There are two kinds of handicap liars. One is the egomaniacal liar. When he is asked his handicap on the first tee for the purpose of arranging a fair wager, he knocks off about five strokes from his real handicap to impress his opponents.

(There is a way egomaniacal liars can actually have handicaps much lower than their actual ability. What you do is this:

Let's say you're fifteen feet away from the hole putting for par. Your partner makes his par, making your putt meaningless as far as the bet is concerned. The egomaniac announces, as his partner's putt goes in, "That makes mine good." He writes down a "4" on his scorecard and winds up shooting thirty-eight on the front having picked up for par on four holes.)

You want to avoid getting an egomaniacal liar as a partner in any form of bet. They will cost you many dollars because they cannot play to their handicap.

Often, partners are decided upon by throwing up each member of a foursome's ball. The two closest balls are one team, the two balls the furthest distance from one another are the other.

When your ball lands near a player who has an ego-reduced handicap, and you know you are going to lose money because of that fact, the smart thing to do is either refuse to play, demand another throwing up of the balls, or say, "If he's a seven, my ass is a typewriter," and perhaps get him more strokes.

If all else fails, hit your partner over the head with your putter, rendering him unconscious and unable to play the round. And go get somebody else.

The other kind of handicap liar is the person who claims his handicap is higher than it actually is. This person is also called a sandbagger, a sandbagging SOB, a cheater, a cheating SOB, a thief, a thieving SOB, or, simply, SOB.

When asked his handicap on the first tee, he will say sixteen.

Sixteen? The sandbagging SOB shot seventy-eight on his own ball in last week's member-guest and he wants sixteen shots?

(There is a way a lying, sandbagging, etc., can actually have a handicap higher than his actual ability, too. Here's how: You are three feet from the hole, putting for par, and your partner rolls in his par putt, making your putt meaningless as far as the bet is concerned.

The LSSOB will then three-putt on purpose and write down "6" on his scorecard, when he easily could have had four. He does this four or five times a round and he's turning in eighty-eights, rather than seventy-eights, keeping his handicap inflated.)

"Why don't we just give you our wallets and you take what you want?" is what to say to somebody who shot seventy-eight on his ball in last week's member-guest, and wants sixteen shots.

You want this person for a partner, if he can get away with getting sixteen shots and can shoot a seventy-eight. If your ball doesn't land next to this player's ball on the first tee, you might say, "Look, it's Halley's Comet!" and while the other players look to the sky, you move your ball next to the one belonging to the sandbagging, etc.

All that said, there is one other matter to discuss on the first tee as the bet and partners are being discussed, and that is extenuating circumstances as in, "I'm a twelve, but I hurt my back having sex with a University of Idaho cheerleader, so I need more strokes."

I've heard some incredible begging for more strokes on the first tee. I was playing with a guy who is a four handicap and he announced on the first tee, "I'm a four, but I'm playing to an eleven. My dog chewed the spikes off my shoes and I can't stay down on the ball."

What golf needs is a system where handicaps are adjusted for such circumstances. I would do so in this way:

• DEATH IN THE FAMILY: Two more strokes a side. It's hard to play golf feeling guilty because you're out on the course while everybody else is at your wife's funeral.

• INJURIES: Shots are added in relation to the creativity one shows while describing the ailment. The old "I-hurt-my-back-while-having-sex-with-a-University-of-Idaho-cheerleader trick will get you an additional shot a side if she was blonde, had big bazoogas and thought Twin Falls was the capital of her home state. "I broke my toe dancing with Juliet Prowse" will get you a couple of strokes, as will, "The little boy had gone down for the third time in icy Lake Michigan when I jumped in, swam over to him and pulled him out of the jaws of death. I've had trouble making a shoulder turn ever since."

• BUSINESS PROBLEMS: Next time you need some more strokes, try saying, "I never should have bought all that Po Folks stock."

• EQUIPMENT: An Arab terrorist stole your sand wedge. An extra shot a side. You broke your seven-iron while attempting to break into a K mart. Two more strokes on the front, one on the back.

• FOREIGN AFFAIRS: "Daniel Ortega is my brother-in-law" should get you a couple of extra shots, as will "My wife is out shopping with Imelda Marcos" or even "I've invited Manuel Noriega to be my partner in the member-guest."

• ACTS OF GOD: "We've been sleeping in the truck since the tornado hit the trailer" is a good one. So is "You should have seen what the sinkhole did to our house in Ponte Vedra."

I've mentioned the term "member-guest" often here, and when discussing various forms of sandbagging, lying and cheating, it becomes necessary to expand a bit on the aforementioned term.

Every golf club has an annual member-guest tournament. This is where you invite a friend, relative, business associate, or your proctologist to be your partner at a tournament at your club. The club charges you several thousand dollars to be in the tournament, but there are free nachos and fried frozen shrimp available after each round, and you get a photograph of you and your partner on the first tee, standing there like a couple of idiots with your drivers.

Each member-guest tournament begins with a calcutta, which works like this:

Everybody in the tournament drinks for a couple of hours and then an auction begins. Each team in the tournament is put up for bids. All the money from the auction goes into a pot.

Let's say you've had six Scotches and you buy Stranglehammer and Forsyth for $1,200. Stranglehammer and Forsyth have the right to give you six hundred dollars for a half interest in themselves.

If Stranglehammer and Forsyth win the member-guest tournament, you and Stranglehammer and Forsyth share forty percent of the pot, which can be a substantial amount of money. Second place brings thirty percent, third brings twenty, and so on until the pot is cleaned out.

With so much money involved – plus, the member-guest winners can gloat – it becomes necessary to cheat if you want to have any chance whatsoever to win and recoup the money your ego forced you to pay for your own team, after first forcing you to drink six Scotches.

Here's how you cheat in a member-guest:

You bring in a ringer. You find somebody from Wyoming who nobody else in the club knows and you invite him to play as your guest. He carries a two handicap, but you claim he's a sixteen when you fill out your entry form for the tournament. That way, he's going to get eight shots a side (if he makes a par on any of the eight holes, it's a net birdie, if he makes a birdie, it's a net eagle, if he makes a hole-in-one on a par three where he gets a shot, you get to write down "0" on your scorecard and the two of you shoot a net forty-three and win the tournament and all the money.)

Most clubs do a tacky thing known as verifying your guest's handicap. That involves your head pro calling the head pro at your guest's club and asking, "Is Marvin Stranglehammer really a sixteen?"

But if you invited somebody from Wyoming, you can say your guest is a sixteen when he's a two, because when your head pro attempts to call your guest's club in Wyoming it will be closed because the entire state is up to its armpits in snow, so you can get away with your clever ruse.

So what happens is on the first day of the tournament, your guest shoots seventy-one on his own ball and you lead the tournament by four hundred shots. When the other participants ask, "How in the hell did that Wyoming SOB shoot seventy-one on his own ball with sixteen shots?" you reply, "Hey, he just made a putt here and there and shot the best round of his life."

The next day, when he shoots sixty-nine on his own ball and you and he win the tournament by seven hundred strokes, you get your check and don't hang around for the cocktail party because nobody else in the tournament knew anybody in Wyoming with a two handicap they could bring in as a sixteen and they want to kill you and the sandbagging SOB you ran in on them.

A traditional team bet is a Nassau – a wager on the front nine holes, the back nine holes and the entire eighteen holes. This is usually a team best ball competition, with handicaps applied. In a five dollar Nassau, a team could win the front one-up, lose the back two-down and therefore lose the eighteen one-down. The net loss is five dollars.

Another typical team bet is "five and two," which means five dollars per side (team best ball with handicaps applied) and two dollars on "trash." In this bet, and sometimes in a Nassau, being two-down automatically freshes the bet, that is, starts a new bet from that point on while the old one continues.

"Trash" is an extra bet and traditionally favors low handicap golfers, but more exotic "trash" makes the game fun for everyone.

The most common trash items are *birdies*, *greenies* (closest to the pin on the first shot on par-three holes, but you must make at least par) and *sandies* (a natural par after being in a sand trap). Obviously low handicap golfers are going to make more birdies, be closer to the pin and make more pars from the sand than higher handicap golfers, so traditional trash items favor the low handicappers.

Less traditional items are more democratic:

SHANKY – a natural par on a hole after shanking a shot.

DIVORCEY – Your wife called you in the grill at the turn and said she was filing for divorce and she wants the house, your car, $2,000 a month in alimony and your dog. If you make par on any hole in the back nine after getting that bit of bad news, it's a piece of trash.

DO-DOEY – If there are animals around your golf course such as cows and geese, and they have, as we discussed earlier, left anything on the green and you have to putt through it and you make the putt, ring the cash register again.

BONKER or WOODY – making par after hitting a tree or limb squarely, thus producing a "bonk" sound. In Florida or other tropical areas, a *Wooshy* is the same thing with a palm tree.

LLOYD BRIDGES – as in "Seahunt." This is where your ball skips across a body of water and you still make par.

PUKEY – You've been up drinking all night, have an early tee time and feel like pond scum. You rush into the woods to puke and return to make par.

I've seen people bet on any number of things on a golf course. While waiting to hit on a tee, I've seen folks bet on trying to chip into the trash can, or putt with their drivers trying to get a ball closest to the tee markers. And I've even seen people bet on a hole played entirely with a putter, from tee to hole.

Two guys in Atlanta (rumor has it they had enjoyed a beer or two) once made a bet on who could play a ball from the clubhouse to a neighborhood bar several miles away in the fewest strokes. The winner played out to the street corner, chipped onto a city bus, rode to the bar, chipped out of the bus and putted into the bar for a four.

Save It For The Jury

A young golf pro struggling to make it on the tour hit a shot into the deep rough. Just as he was about to chip back to the fairway, a frog hopped out of the bushes and spoke to him. "Hey, fellow," said the frog, "if you'd move your left hand back just a little, you'd be a great golfer."

The young pro looked at the frog and said, "What the hell do you know about golf? You're just a stupid frog."

"Trust me," said the frog. →

With little to lose, the pro took the frog's advice and hit a great recovery shot. He put the frog in his bag and went on to play a brilliant round. Taking the frog's advice, he won that tournament and five others before the end of the year. He was the leading money winner on the PGA tour and one of the world's best golfers.

One day the frog, who had been with him the whole time, said, "After all I've done for you, I want you to do something for me."

"What's that?" asked the golfer.

"I want you to kiss me," said the frog.

"Kiss you? I ain't kissing no slimey frog," said the golf pro. But finally he had to admit he owed the frog a great debt, and if a kiss was the payback, he couldn't refuse. So he kissed the frog flush on the lips.

To his surprise, the frog suddenly turned into a beautiful, naked fourteen-year-old girl. Lying nude on the bed, she said, "Now I want you to make love to me."

"I can't do that," said the golf pro. "You're beautiful, but you're much too young."

"After all I've done for you, you would refuse me this one request?" said the young girl.

So the golfer relented and made love to her.

"And, Your Honor, that's exactly how it happened!"

"I don't know about that new pro," said Dave. "He may be a little strange."

"Why do you think that?" asked Clyde.

"He just tried to correct my stance again."

"So?" said Clyde. "He's just trying to help your game."

"Yeah, I know," said Dave, "but I was standing at the urinal at the time."

***

Fred, an obstetrician, and James, a recent first-time father, had been golfing buddies for years, but James was furious about a bill he had just received from Fred.

"How can you charge $200 for use of the delivery room when you know good and well that Alice delivered the baby on the front lawn of the hospital?" James ranted.

"You're right," said Fred as he took the bill from James. He scratched out the words "Delivery Room Fee" and wrote in "Greens Fee."

Why Are There No Republicans on Public Courses?

In the years since I sneaked on to the Athens Country Club course, my first taste of a private club, I have been fortunate enough to play at many others.

I once played at a club so exclusive you had to have suffered your second heart attack before you could join. The average age of the members was deceased.

Of course, only a couple of clubs in the world are as exclusive as the Augusta National Golf Club in Augusta, Georgia, site of the Masters tournament. Since it is truly a national club and the local membership is no more than thirty or so, and invitations to guests are limited, members say it is sometimes difficult for members to find a game.

There is a true story which demonstrates the point:

One beautiful fall Saturday during football season, a National member decided he would love to play golf. He called the club looking for a game, but no one had scheduled a tee time. Several phone calls later, he still couldn't find anyone to play.

Finally, he called a friend and said, "How would you like to be my guest for a round of golf today?"

"Great," said the friend.

"Excellent. I've reserved the Augusta National course for us." They were, in fact, the only golfers on the course that day. Now *that's* ex-by-God-clusive.

* * *

After years of arduous research, I have come up with a list of ways to distinguish public courses from private courses. I offer these for the personal enrichment of my readers:

• Players on private courses acknowledge good shots by saying, "Nice swing, Edward." Players on public courses say, "You lucky mutha!"

• The rough on private courses is usually cut to precisely three inches. Depending on the type of grass, that can leave very difficult shots. For example, the rough at U.S. Open courses is like Roach Motels – you check in but you don't check out. You may find similar rough on public courses, but there it is the result of a broken bush-hog rather than strategic design.

• The balls from the practice range of the private club later become pro shop inventory at the public course.

• At private courses they'll shine your street shoes while you play. At public courses they'll steal your street shoes while you play. I know there's at least one person with taste at my club because he stole my Guccis.

• Golf carts at private clubs sound like electric fans. Carts at public courses sound like '56 Chevys with dual exhausts and glass packs.

• Finer private clubs will have a wine bar. Most public clubhouses have a wino in a corner sleeping off a drunk.

• The masseuse at private clubs will give you a rub-down. Anybody who tries that at a public course is usually light in his loafers or out on bail.

• At private courses, men restrict the days and times when women can play. At public courses, wives usually decide when husbands can play.

• Golfers at private clubs ask, "May we play through?" At public courses they hit first and ask questions later.

• At private courses, they play it as it lies. At public courses, they play it as it lays and then lie.

• Starters on private courses are usually retired executives. Starters on public courses are usually off-duty cops.

Charlie and Bruce, both low handicappers, were flying around the course and having a great round until they ran up behind two women playing together. Suddenly they had to wait before every shot.

"I think I'll walk up and ask them if we can play through," said Charlie.

"Good idea," said Bruce.

Charlie walked about fifty yards towards the women, made a quick U-turn and headed back for Bruce.

"I thought you were going to ask them if we could play through," said Bruce.

"I was," said Charlie, "but when I got close enough to see them, I realized that's my wife playing golf with my mistress."

"Are you sure? Let me go take a look," said Bruce. He walked thirty or forty yards down the fairway, did a quick about-face and came back to Charlie. "What a coincidence," he said.

How To Improve Your Lie Without Getting Caught in One

Cheating in golf can range from subtle to blatant, from nominal to heinous. The universal law of relativity (discovered by either Dow Finsterwald or Albert Einstein, I forget which) dictates which it is: If *you* are doing the cheating, it usually doesn't amount to much . . . certainly not anything you'd have to worry about on Sunday morning. But if your opponent is cheating, it's likely to be a capital offense. Punishment for getting caught is being publicly humiliated in the men's grill and being forced to play with your wife in the next mixed couple tournament.

I, of course, have very little hands-on experience in this area. But in my endless quest for truth, justice and new tips for lowering my handicap, I have conducted extensive interviews with known cheaters and can now share some of their techniques with you.

(You must be over eighteen or have the consent of a parent or guardian to read beyond this point.)

MOVING VIOLATION

The most common form of cheating on the golf course is moving the ball in the rough. Even when you're playing winter rules, which allow the ball to be repositioned in the fairway, you're still not supposed to touch the ball in the rough.

But what if you're directly behind a tree, or an overhanging limb obstructs your swing, and just a foot or so in either direction would give you relief? On a four-hundred-yard hole, what difference does twelve inches make?

There are two techniques widely used for moving the ball in the rough. One is to wait until your playing partners are a safe distance away, squat down like you're removing an unattached and non-living object from around your ball, and quickly move it the necessary foot.

The other technique is to wait until someone else actually hits their shot. At that moment, all eyes usually are on the ball. Yours, however, should be on *your* ball as you gently kick it to a better line.

Neither of these techniques works if your opponents don't trust you and therefore follow you in the woods and wait for you to hit your shot before moving on to theirs. That's usually a sign that you've gone to the well for a good line one time too often.

Should you ever get caught moving your ball in the rough, your first response should be, "My ball was sitting on a rock, and I'm not ruining a club over a five-dollar bet." If that doesn't work, try, "Hey, I thought this was a friendly game." Then act indignant and try to shift the guilt.

FINDERS KEEPERS, LOSERS WEEPERS

Another popular form of cheating is finding lost balls. Say you hit a shot into the woods. After several minutes of looking, it becomes obvious that you're probably not going to find your ball, that your opponents are probably going to win the hole by default, and that you'll probably have to get a night job to pay off the bet.

What to do? If you planned ahead, you have a replacement ball on your person and can suddenly "find" it in a place not totally cleared (nobody would believe that) but with a shot toward the fairway or green.

There are several methods for actually getting the ball on the ground. One is to have it in your pocket when you walk into the woods, pull it out, announce that you found it and simultaneously place it on the ground as you dramatically brush away surrounding debris. The only problem here is that the replacement ball may be visible between your pocket and the ground.

One way to minimize this risk is to have a hole cut in one of your pockets (remember which one before you put your car keys or loose change in there). As you search the woods for your ball, the replacement can slip through the hole in your pocket, fall down your pants leg and roll out into a nice lie.

In cool weather, when you're probably wearing a sweater or wind breaker, another technique is to have the ball inside the sleeve on the inside of your wrist (where you take your pulse). Then you yell, "Here it is!" and as you reach down, the ball falls from your sleeve.

In all cases, be sure to pick a soft spot so the ball doesn't roll when it hits the ground.

There are also several other points to remember. For example, don't take a *new* replacement ball into the woods if you've been playing with an old one. In fact, it's best to have the same kind of ball and even better to have the same numbered ball.

Also, don't take a yellow replacement ball into the woods if you're looking for a white one. That tends to be a dead giveaway.

Finally, there's a story about this situation which brings up an interesting moral question: A golfer hit his shot into the woods, and his partner and two opponents were helping him look for it. One opponent whispers to the other, "He'll never find this one."

"How do you know that?" asks his companion.

"Because I've got it in my pocket."

About that time, their opponent yells, "Here it is!"

Do you call him a liar and explain how you know?

Didn't the same thing happen somewhere in the Old Testament? Was Adam really holding an half-eaten apple behind his back when he accused Eve?

I never knew golf was so philosophical.

MARK AND REMARK

Cheating on the greens requires far more finesse than cheating in the woods because everyone is there and, unless you're playing with Mr. Magoo, can watch you closer.

The easiest and most common cheat is mismarking your ball by picking it up first and then tossing down a mark. It's the golf equivalent of the game tossing to the line. With practice, you can make a dime roll eight or nine inches closer to the hole before it settles down.

Another method is using two markers. First you properly mark your ball, then two or three steps closer to the hole you casually drop another mark. When it comes your time to putt, you place your ball on the marker nearest to the hole. If you choose this method, mark with pennies; leaving dimes behind could get expensive.

And don't forget that these marking techniques can be used in reverse against your opponents. Wasn't that nice of you to mark their balls while they were making their way to the green? Isn't it funny how a putt that looks only six or seven feet long from the fairway is really fifteen feet when you get to the green?

GRAFFITI

On most golf courses, a white circle indicates Ground Under Repair. Any ball that lands inside can be repositioned outside the circle without penalty.

For those rare occasions when you get a bad lie or a bad line, a small can of spray paint in your pocket or in your bag can create instant Ground Under Repair and provide the necessary relief. How do you spell PAR?

TEED OFF

How you ever tried hitting a driver out of the rough? Every time I've tried it, the resulting shot killed forty-seven earth worms and left a trench in the ground.

So how is it that occasionally somebody, usually my opponent, hits a driver from the rough better than he hit it off the tee? How? I'll tell you how. He teed it up. Oldest trick in the book. Some things can't be improved upon, not even by technology.

4 + 2 = 5

When I finish a round of golf, I can tell you where every shot I hit went. And most times I can tell you where every one of my opponents' shots went.

So why is it that some guys can't remember how many swings they took on one hole? You've seen them. They hack it around from tee to green, then make two passes at the cup before picking up a six-footer. I already know what they made on the hole, but just for sport I ask.

"Let's see," says Sir Isaac Newton, "I was one in the woods, two under the bush, three in the trap, four on the green and two putts for six."

"Actually you were three in the woods. That first drive you hit out of bounds carries a stroke and distance penalty."

"Penalty? It's penalty enough that I lost that ball. But I want to play by the rules, so make it an eight."

"What about the shot you banked off that passing car?"

"Oh, yeah. Nine."

"And what about that first sand shot you left in the trap?"

"Did I? Yeah, that's right. Ten."

"And you made that last six-foot putt?"

"Well, sure, you know I don't miss those."

What I do know is that the man's math is worse than Ivan Boesky's.

WAS THAT A FORWARD LATERAL?

When I was growing up, the Ford Motor Company used to sponsor a national Punt, Pass and Kick competition. I think some of the guys I play golf with must have been finalists in that contest.

Punting, passing and kicking all are methods of cheating as long as you do them while no one is watching. Like in extramarital sex.

LYING OF FLIGHT

When a golfer hits a shot into a water hazard, he is supposed to take a one-shot penalty and place the ball on the same line that it went into the water and no closer to the hole.

I remember something from my high school geometry class that comes into play here, something that I probably asked at the time: "How will I ever use that silly information in real life?" As divergent lines go out from a point, the distance between them increases as their length increases.

What that means is this: You hit your drive into the water on the right side of the fairway. From the tee you chose a marker, usually a tree or something in the distance, that is on the same line as your ball was. If, however, enroute to your ball you were to get your trees mixed up, you could end up placing your ball thirty yards closer to the hole. "Yeah, I had it lined up on this tree right here," you say to your skeptical opponents.

Another favorite trick of mine is to line up my ball on a bird. Nine times out of ten they'll fly away before I get there, and I have to remember where they were.

THE CHECKERED FLAG

Finally, one of the keys to successful cheating is choosing a fast golf cart. Get the picture: Your foursome is on the tee when you hit a drive near a hazard. Someone asks, "Is it in the creek?"

What you think but don't dare say is, "Not if I get there first."

You and your partner jump into your cart while your opponents clamber into theirs. If you get to the ball well ahead of them, the odds that your ball is *not* in the creek increase dramatically.

I have found that a small tip, usually two to three dollars, to the cartmaster before teeing off is a good investment. It's amazing how often my opponents get carts that barely make it around the course, while mine run like they were built by Maserati.

Fred had tried to be particularly careful about his language as he played golf with his preacher. But on the twelfth hole, when he twice failed to hit out of a sand trap, he lost his resolve and let fly with a string of expletives.

The preacher felt obliged to respond. "I have observed," said he in a calm voice, "that the best golfers do not use foul language."

"I guess not. What the hell do they have to cuss about?"

I'm Not Saying They Were Slow, But Winter In Chicago Was Quicker

Slow play is the bane of good golfers. After following a particularly slow elderly gentleman for seven holes without being invited to play through, a younger man yelled, "Could you speed it up just a little bit?"

The old man yelled back, "I'll have you to know that I was playing this game before you were born."

"That's fine and good," said the younger golfer, "but I'd be obliged if you'd try to finish it before I die."

***

In certain parts of the world, most notably Scotland, an average round of golf takes only about three hours. Scottish golfers tend to play quickly because they're generally good and because they're trying to finish before the next squall comes ashore.

The average round in America takes approximately four and one-half hours, unless, of course, you're playing a resort course, in which case the average time is about six agonizing hours.

I used to think that slow play could be attributed directly to televised golf. Joe Bologna, a twenty-six handicapper, sits at home and watches the pros play on television. They discuss the shots with their caddies, take a couple of practice swings, and hit the shots. Then when they get to the green, they study their putts from all sides, step up, and knock it close if not in.

Joe watches this and figures, "Hey, if that's the way the pros do it and shoot even par, I'll do the same and shave some shots off my score." So the next time he plays, Joe discusses his shot with his partner, takes a couple of practice swings, and hits the shot . . . about twenty yards to the right.

He gets in the cart, drives twenty yards, changes clubs, discusses the shot with his partner, and hits it again . . . this time about thirty-five yards to the left.

Five shots later, following more discussion than an international summit, Joe reaches the green. He's got a forty-foot, uphill putt; odds are he'll win the lottery before he makes this putt. But, just as he saw on television, he studies the putt from all sides, sets up, and hits it halfway to the hole. Now he again studies the putt from every angle, sets up, and knocks it fifteen feet past the cup. Finally Joe scrapes it in the hole for a natural eleven. Have you ever noticed how slow play becomes the week after the Masters has been on television?

In recent years, however, I have decided that televised golf is only part of the slow play problem. The rest, I conclude, can be attributed to (1) nouveau riche foreigners, (2) company tournaments, (3) Canadian and Yankee tourists and (4) women.

I took a couple of weeks off not long ago and went to one of my favorite Southern golf resorts, the Hyatt Grand Cypress in Orlando.

There are forty-five holes at Grand Cypress, eighteen of which make up one of my favorite Southern golf courses, The New Course.

The New Course is named that because its designer, Jack Nicklaus, tried to make it look and play like The Old Course in St. Andrews, Scotland. I have played The Old Course in St. Andrews, and The New Course at Grand Cypress could be its cousin. First cousin.

There are the dreaded pot bunkers just like St. Andrews, and a burn, which is Scottish for creek, runs throughout the course and eats golf balls.

As much as I enjoy Grand Cypress and The New Course, I encountered four of the five main reasons for slow play. Here's a hint: My round was not televised. If it had been, Jerry Lewis would have been there raising money for some charity. We're talking telethon. Marathon. Homicide. Suicide.

Obstacle No. 1 was the recently wealthy foreigners. Grand Cypress charges about a hundred big ones for a round of golf. This, of course, is nothing for people who pay the equivalent of the GNP of a Third World country just to play back home.

So they descend on such resorts as Grand Cypress, buy out the pro shop and play from dawn to dusk. That's how long it takes them to complete eighteen holes.

A guy who worked at another Orlando golf course told me that four foreign guys who showed up to play had leased a local television station's helicopter; it hovered over them for eighteen holes, videotaping every shot, as seen from three hundred feet above.

I got behind a Japanese foursome at The New Course. Not only did they take five-and-a-half hours to play, but when I suggested they speed things up a bit, they handed me a camera and asked me to take their picture. Then they took one of me and told me if ever I were in Tokyo to give them a call and they would arrange a game for me, provided I could qualify for a substantial loan at the Bank of Tokyo.

Obstacle No. 2 was a company tournament. Many companies hold their annual conventions at Southern golf resorts in the winter, not to mention their annual company golf tournaments.

Here's how it works: The company president gets up at the Registration and Welcome cocktail party and says, "Tomorrow is our annual company golf tournament, and we'd like a good turnout.

"It doesn't matter if you don't play golf. We're just out for a good time, so come on along and join us. There will be lots of beer on the course."

Six zillion furniture salesmen hit the course the next day, and your tee time is always just after the last foursome in the tournament goes off.

Prepare for another six-hour round. One of the few things that moves slower than a company golf tournament is winter in Chicago. On my second day at The New Course, I played behind the National Association of Tank Truck Owners.

There was a twosome playing out of one bag. There was a guy who whiffed it three times on one tee and then threw the ball fifty yards down the fairway. There he whiffed it three more times, and I cursed the sun.

When I arrived at the seventeenth tee, there were two foursomes waiting to hit. So everybody started spraying everybody else with beer.

As I stood over a putt at the seventeenth three days later, one of the guys in the foursome that was departing asked me, "Hey buddy, whar's eighteen?"

"In Palatka," I answered. I missed my putt.

Obstacle No. 3 was the dreaded Canadian or Yankee tourist, down from Cleveland or Detroit or some god-awful place in New Jersey or Toronto. You can recognize them by the way they dress for the golf course. Look for white legs with no hair on them. Look for tennis shorts and black stretch socks pulled up as close to their armpits as they can get them. Look for silly hats.

I saw a Yankee tourist playing golf in a pair of tennis shorts, black socks and a long-sleeve shirt. He was the best dresser in his foursome.

The fifteenth hole at The New Course is a par five, eight hundred yards long. There is water on the hole, not to mention a pot bunker every six yards and then a bunker down by the green that is large enough to film a scene from *Lawrence of Arabia*. I am convinced Jack Nicklaus's wife was having PMS cramps when he designed the fifteenth at The New Course.

So my foursome, all Southerners, had been behind these four Yankee honkers all afternoon. Cross-town traffic in Manhattan moves faster than they played, for God's sake.

When we arrived at the fifteenth, they hadn't teed off yet. "Y'all haven't teed off yet?" I asked.

"It's the foursome ahead of us," said one of the honkers, who was wearing a silly hat. I looked at his bag and there was a tag from some course in New Jersey.

"Do you mean," I said, "the foursome that is walking off the fifteenth green three miles ahead of you?"

"They're slow," he said. "Very slow." (Yankee golfers are bad to repeat themselves.)

They finally teed off. One topped it fifty yards and didn't make the ladies' tee. We thought of explaining the Ft. Worth Rule to him, but then we thought better of it. It would only slow things down more.

The next guy hit it in the water on the right. The next went into a pot bunker, and the fourth hit his in the monkey grass which guards the left side of the fairway.

We timed it. Twenty-eight minutes after the Yankees teed off, they were out of range so we could hit our drives.

A guy in my foursome who lives in Orlando said, "If the SOBs didn't come down here and spend all that money, there'd be a bounty on 'em."

A lot of Southern golf resorts have alligators. Alligators do not know how much money Yankee tourists spend. So there is some hope.

Obstacle No. 4 was women. I once wrote in a column that women should have their own golf courses so they wouldn't slow down male players. Lady golfers at my home course burned a sand wedge in front of my locker, and my secretary, the lovely and talented Miss Wanda Fribish, who is also an officer in the 303rd Bombadier Wing of the National Organization for Livid Women, said, "Die, scumbag!" as she threw her daggerlike letter opener at me.

Luckily, I was able to dodge her missile. It stuck in the photograph of the October playmate that hangs on my wall.

Perhaps I should attempt to clear up my stand on women on the golf course:

First, there are many, many women who can beat me playing golf. I am to golf what Moammar Khadafy is to world peace. Who I'm talking about are the female versions of me, the lady hackers. They are the ones who slow down play, and here is why:

When the male high-handicapper reaches a score of double-bogey or triple-bogey and he still doesn't have the ball in the hole, he avoids further embarrassment by moving on to the next hole so as not to slow down golfers behind him. Not so with many women high-handicappers. They are resolved to get the ball into the hole regardless of how many strokes it takes.

I was playing behind a woman at Grand Cypress. After she took two hours to complete the first six holes, I counted her strokes on the seventh.

She made a twenty-six. It was a par three.

Men and women could get along on the same golf course if women simply would PUT THE DANG BALL IN THEIR POCKETS AND MOVE ON AFTER THEIR SCORE REACHES DOUBLE DIGITS.

This will never happen, of course, which is why women should have their own golf courses so they can hack the ball around as long as their hearts desire. Women have their own restrooms and bridge clubs, don't they? So what's wrong with their own golf courses?

As far as Ms. October is concerned, she was hit by the letter opener in such a location that she certainly won't be playing golf anytime soon.

***

There is this place in south Florida – I can't tell you the name of it or exactly where it is – where they have solved the problem of women on the golf course. The reason I'm not going to put a name or location on it is because some feminist might read this and decide to file suit, and I might never be invited back as a guest.

At this golf club, women are not only forbidden from the course, they aren't even allowed on the grounds except once a year. For the annual Christmas party.

Your wife drives you to the club. She lets you off at the front gate. Phone calls from women are even discouraged.

"And you can play gin rummy naked," a member explained to me. I'm not certain I'd want to play gin rummy naked, but I saw the member's point.

There aren't any women within miles of the club, so you're safe to belch or curse or make funny noises with your armpit, or, if you so desire, to play gin rummy naked.

"When will men ever grow up and get over such as this?" flared-nostril women readers are asking.

Most of us never will because of the Treehouse Syndrome. When men are boys, they build treehouses, or other assorted edifices, in order to have a secret place to go with their friends where there aren't any girls to tell them how stupid they are, or how they should move the orange crate over near the cardboard box that serves as a table in order to give the room more symmetry.

We need this getaway all our lives in order to gather our wits and share the goodness that is brotherhood.

And to play gin rummy naked if we want to.

Men have given up so much of what was once their exclusive space as it is. And some of it we needed to share. Like boardrooms and mastheads and offices on the top floor.

But at this club at least, men have drawn the line at golf.

"What I like most about this club," said a friend who was also a guest, "is there aren't any ladies' tees. You can hit from all the way up front and not feel like a wimp."

Indeed.

***

My own baptism in the necessity of picking up came when, after nearly a decade away from the game, I launched my comeback at Myrtle Beach, South Carolina. A companion and I paid a week's salary for green fees, rental clubs, electric cart and a half-dozen golf balls. (I could have sworn they were white when I quit playing.)

On the first tee my playing partner and I made the obligatory small wager and then proceeded to tee off. Unfortunately, my first drive sliced into the backyard of somebody's condominium where a Tupperware party was in progress. I got a free container suitable for serving congealed salads and a free drop off the coffee table.

My second shot, a three wood, caught a tree limb and bounced back toward the Tupperware party, coming to rest on a plate of cheese and crackers the ladies were munching with their white wine. This time I bought six cups and a casserole container to pay for the damages and pitched back into the fairway. I took a twelve on the first hole. My companion went one-up with an eleven. We agreed to pick up before we reached double digits again.

We both went into the water on the second hole – the water in a swimming pool located behind somebody else's condominium where a woman sat reading a copy of *Cosmopolitan*. My companion removed his tennis shorts and waded into the pool to retrieve our errant shots. The woman went inside and fetched her husband, a very large man who threatened to call the authorities if we weren't off his property within thirty seconds.

In our haste to leave, we drove the cart over one of the pool chairs, which wouldn't have been all that bad had it not been the one the woman was sitting in at the time. Luckily, the poor woman was unhurt, but her *Cosmo* got caught under one of the cart wheels, and we scattered a series on unsightly liver spots for several hundred yards. I finally shot a sixty-six on the front nine. My companion had a sixty-two and took me for a dollar.

Undaunted, we drove to the strip on Myrtle Beach and got in a quick eighteen holes at Jungle Jim's Carpet Golf, where they don't care if you take off your shirt just as long as you don't steal the scoring pencils.

Relieved to get away from the pressure of the regular links, I got my dollar back on the last hole by sinking a long putt that rolled into the monkey's mouth, out through his tail, then under the giraffe's legs before dropping squarely into the cup. It must have been finishing on that high note that brought me back to the game for good. Or bad. Or whatever.

No Matter What You Call It, It Still Goes Sideways

There are certain words in every environment that are inappropriate. For example, you probably shouldn't talk about your favorite *Kool-Aid* flavor at a convention of Jim Jones followers. At a brith milah ceremony, you shouldn't brag about the new *carving set* you bought your wife. You never mention the words *no-hitter* when a baseball pitcher is actually throwing one, and you most certainly never say the S-word to a golfer.

The S-word is the most dreaded of all golf diseases because there is no known cure, short of a frontal lobotomy, which tends to have an adverse effect on other parts of the golf game. Like remembering how to get to the course. Or what to do when you get there.

The S-word is like a cancer that grows slowly in the golfer's brain. Even on days when you feel great and are playing well, it lurks in the recesses of your mind, just waiting for the chance to strike. To spread. To drive you looney.

The word itself is so intimidating that golfers have created many euphemisms for it:

- Chinese hook
- lateral
- three o'clock
- snap fade
- power push
- "thang"

Although many teaching professionals claim to be able to cure the S-word, those afflicted with the disease say it ain't so. Not even the CDC has been able to wipe out this scourge of golf.

The only thing we all know for sure is that the shot is created by hitting the ball with the hosel of the club. This can be done by leaving the club face open or by closing it. One way or the other, the ball makes contact with the hosel instead of the club face.

There are stories of pros being driven from the tour by the S-word. My club pro told me about a man who came to him in tears because of the S-word. A good friend of mine, Boom-Boom Boyd, who played on his college golf team and has actually won a legitimate golf tournament in his career, contracted the disease a couple of years ago and has been struggling since.

When I told him I was writing a chapter for this book on the S-word, he offered a personal testimony about what it's like to suffer this fate. His hope is that by sharing his experience, others may be spared the same humiliation . . . or at least give him more shots next time they're making a bet:

"The S-word is a life-altering disease. In one quick flash of flexible steel, your entire personality and outlook on existence is changed for all eternity.

"You are embarrassed; you are emasculated; you are stripped naked of all self-worth. You lose control of your private bodily functions, sometimes on the very spot. It is the sensation of being struck with a cold bolt of lightning. It sends a flash of nausea through your entire body, churning your bowels.

"You immediately look for a place to hide, but it is hopeless. To relieve the pain and embarrassment, your soul seeks to leave your body. You see Jesus in reverse.

"You are panicked. You consider surgery. A sex change operation is not ruled out.

"My experience leads me to conclude that the S-word is not a physical disease but rather a spiritual sickness. Somewhat akin to demonic possession. Could I have committed some travesty in an earlier life that would warrant this type of punishment?

"The S-word is contagious, so your golfing comrades avoid you. You go to your club. The parking lot is filled with automobiles, but no one is inside. You are reminded of the closing scene from the movie *On the Beach*. You search the premises for your friends, and, alas, find them huddled and trembling in the far corner of the locker room hiding in a darkened shower stall.

"Life seems hopeless. But it goes on.

"There are more remedies for the S-word than there are cures for the common cold, and all are equally ineffective. Yet in desperation you try them all. Eventually you seek professional assistance. Your local teaching pro promises to cure you. In fifty-five years of golf, he says, he has never S-worded a golf ball. The fundamentals of the golf swing were instilled in him at a very early age by his father, who was also a professional.

"After two hours on the practice tee, you have given him the disease.

"Word of your trouble is spreading. It has reached a friend who is a touring professional. He calls to offer help. On a break from the tour, he meets you on the practice tee one Sunday afternoon. He watches you S-word practice balls for the better part of an hour without comment. Then he asks if you might be able to teach him the shot to be used as a psychological weapon in Australian match play.

"You are awakened at night by a dreamy remedy. Could this be a heavenly vision? You slip silently from your bed in hopes that you do not awaken your wife, who is sleeping in a deep state of exhaustion brought on as a result of having to carry the entire financial burden of providing for the family during your illness.

"You put on your golf shoes in the darkness and stuff whiffle balls into your bathrobe pockets. You take your wedge outside and experiment with the newfound solution. In the headlights of your automobile, on your small front lawn, it works! You rush inside and euphorically call your pro from his sleep to analyze the experience.

"His conclusion: 'If the whiffle balls are going straight, then you need to start playing the sons of bitches.'

"I remain bowed but not broken. Like so many others, I must survive until a cure is discovered."

Don't it just break your heart? A man stricken in his prime. But fate is a cruel mistress.

This same poor soul was part of our group which went to Scotland to play golf for two weeks. Before our first round, my friend went to the men's locker room to relieve himself. Suddenly we heard a blood-curdling scream and rushed in to find him standing there paralyzed. On the front of every urinal, dyed into the porcelain like fine Wedgewood china, was the name of the manufacturer – Armitage Shanks.

The justice of the peace in a small town was about to tee off with two other friends one day when the club pro volunteered to join them. It seemed like the perfect opportunity for a free lesson. But instead of being helpful, the pro was openly critical of the JP's game. At every bumbled shot, the pro made a joke about the justice.

But the criticism didn't even stop at the end of the round. The pro continued to embarrass the JP in the clubhouse among his friends. Finally the pro got up to leave and said, "Judge, let's do it again sometime. If you can't find anybody else to make it a foursome, I'll be glad to play with you again."

The justice of the peace said, "How about next Saturday? I don't think any of my friends can join us, so why don't you invite your parents, and after our round I could marry them."

An Italian, a Frenchman and a Scotsman were playing golf on a links course when they spotted a stunning mermaid on the shore. They all dropped their clubs and ran down for a closer look.

The mermaid was incredibly beautiful and voluptuous. The Italian, burning with desire, asked the mermaid, "Have you ever been fondled?"

"No, I haven't," whispered the mermaid. So the Italian walked over and hugged and fondled her warmly. The mermaid said, "Hmmmm, that's nice."

The Frenchman, not to be outdone, said, "Have you ever been kissed?"

"No, I haven't," answered the mermaid. So the Frenchman went over and kissed her long and slow. "Hmmmm," sighed the mermaid, "that's nice."

Finally the Scotsman asked her, "Have you ever been screwed?"

"No, I haven't," said the mermaid.

"Well, you have now," said the Scotsman, "'cause the tide's out!"

The Firths, Fourths and Fifths of Foreign Golf

I have played tennis in three foreign countries. Except for an occasional sign in a strange tongue, usually forbidding spitting or playing without a shirt, the experiences were identical. I don't remember one overhead from another, because the tennis court, by design, is the same in Europe as it is America.

I also have played golf in three foreign countries – four, if you count Hawaii. Each experience was unique, each course different, each round memorable. The only thing that was the same in each instance was the caliber of my game, which is beside the point.

That's one of the glories of golf. Every course you play – whether domestic or foreign, public or private, long or short, mountain or beach – is a new and wonderful experience. Even bad courses usually have a couple of great holes on them.

In addition to the courses being different throughout the world, the nuances surrounding the game also are different. Nowhere are they more distinct than in Scotland, the birthplace of golf and the site of my ancestral home – Glen Close.

***

Twice I have been to Scotland with a group of golfers to play the most historic courses in the world. Each time I came back a bloody pulp but never more in love with the game.

It's amazing to me that any American golfer has ever won the British Open, because the courses and the elements are so unlike ours that it's almost a different game.

Maybe that's what my caddy meant one trying day when I said, "I want you to know this is not the game I usually play." He answered, "I should hope not, sir. But tell me, what game do you usually play?"

The links courses of Ireland and Scotland are topographical wonders. Situated next to bays (sometimes called firths, a Scottish word for "large water hazard") or directly next to the ocean, they are always windblown. And rain-blown.

You've heard the old joke: If you don't like the weather, just hang around a few minutes and it'll change. That joke must have originated near a links course.

One day at Lahinch in Ireland, we teed off in beautiful Irish weather (that means cloudly, fifty degrees, and winds gusting up to thirty miles an hour).

Before we finished nine holes, the wind was at gale force and rain was blowing horizontally. My caddy, a nine-year-old boy, could no longer move forward into the

MAY I
PLAY
THRU

wind, so I had to abandon him and carry my clubs the rest of the way. I hope the nice lad was found.

I had my doubts about him before we even started. The first tip that the youngster might have trouble was the fact that he was barely taller than my bag. I complained to the caddymaster about having a nine-year-old boy as a caddy.

"Better to have them very young, sir," said the caddymaster. "The lad probably can't count past ten."

By the time I finally left him on the course, he looked and walked like Walter Brennan. Bad golf will age a man – or boy – quickly.

I finished the round, of course. That's part of the thrill of Irish and Scottish golf. No matter what the elements, you persevere. One of our group, leaning into the wind at a forty-five degree angle, yelled, "Next time there's a hurricane warning off the Georgia coast, why don't we call down and get tee times for the group?"

Another member of our group had washed a pair of pants in the hotel the night before. He apparently had not rinsed them very well, however, because as the rain soaked through his pants, they began sudsing. Every time the man took a step, suds bubbled out of his shoes. And from between his legs. It looked like he had taken an Oxydol enema.

The wind blew so hard that you couldn't spot a ball on the green without its blowing. If you were downwind, you didn't even have to hit the putt; you just spotted it and let it go. If you were upwind, you had to make an indentation in the green and place the ball in it, and then you had to take a full shoulder turn to drive the putt into the wind.

At the Old Course at St. Andrews, Scotland, the wind was gusting to fifty miles per hour. My caddy said, "Aye, sir, you should be here when the wind really gets up." Moments later, as he handed me a club for a shot into the teeth of the wind, he said, "Best to keep it low, sir." Oh, really?

Beautiful and intimidating land formations are created by these elements. No bulldozer has ever set tread here. Huge mounds rise up in the middle of fairways, and cliffs are formed by the pounding of the sea. Pot bunkers – deep, hellish depressions all over the courses – were created by sheep seeking shelter from the wind and rain. Three hundred years ago, that's all this land was good for – grazing sheep. And then some sadistic soul designed a golf course on it. They left the natural bunkers and, not content with mere punishment, even added sand in the bottom of some of them.

There's a joke about one of the bunkers at Muirfield in Scotland which tells the story:

One day a priest playing the fabled course found himself with an impossible lie in one of the deep fairway bunkers. His ball was buried in sand and the wall of the bunker was four feet high.

The priest looked at his ball, turned his face toward Heaven and said, "God, help me." Then he looked back at the ball, the part of it that was showing, turned again to Heaven and said, "And, God, don't send Jesus. This is no shot for a boy!"

Amen.

***

Unlike in America, most of these wonderful courses are open to the public. Nonetheless, I recommend that you travel with a golfing group if possible because a lot of things can go wrong between Ireland and Scotland, as you'll soon read.

Since portions of these trips are not perfectly clear in my memory (must have been something in the water . . . or over the ice), I have asked my friend and erstwhile correspondent, Mikey "The Mouse" Steed, playing out of the Social Circle Sewing Center in Ft. Deposit, Alabama, to offer advice to any aspiring masochist who wants to play golf in Ireland and Scotland. You're up, Mike.

"When contemplating such a trip, you can make no more important decision than who is going. Choose wisely those companions you enjoy, because ten days at close quarters will test friendships.

Our group was led (astray, most often) by Lewis McDonald Grizzard, "a legend under the kilt," as he told us frequently. The group consisted of redneck racconteurs, good old boys and middle-aged professionals (Muppies). You know the type – they hang around bars, playing gin and telling lies.

The coveted invitations were extended to almost anyone who could gather enough money to put up a deposit and produce a handicap of fifteen or below, which is required for play on many Scottish courses.

Seeking a name that blended the character of the group with the homeland of golf (where everything is either "Royal" or "McSomething"), we named our event "The McNeck Invitational." The runner-up name was

"Floggers of the Firth of Feces." Rejection of that name was the final display of good taste exhibited by the travelers.

ARRANGEMENTS

There are many good tour operators who specialize in golf packages that are nearly idiot proof. We tested this claim and found it to be true. They book the flights, the hotels, transfers, and, most importantly, the tee times.

Both times we were graced by the world's best bus driver, Scotsman Tommy Hanlon, who told some of the best and raunchiest jokes we ever heard. Usually by the third telling of a joke, we caught enough of his Scottish brogue to understand it. He also taught us local swearing and got us to the course on time.

It was Tommy who, when questioned about the existence of the Loch Ness monster, said, "Of course I believe in her. I divorced her only six months ago."

WOMEN

Your trip likely will be celibate unless you bring your own. There just aren't that many women around the golf courses in Scotland and Ireland . . . and those who are there are difficult to distinguish from the ubiquitous sheep.

Without mentioning any names, one member of our group was always attempting to befriend attractive desk clerks and waitresses. Lewis's first move was to ask a comely lassie her name. She might reply, "My name is Abigail." From there the exchange was predictable.

"Ah, Abigail, what a lovely name. Are you married?"

"Yes."

"And are you happily married?"

The man was persistent if not successful. After awhile, I devised a plan to help keep this dog under the porch. I learned that nearly half of the Irish people speak Gaelic and virtually all understand it. I learned a Gaelic phrase from my Irish caddy at Ballybunion which goes, "Pog ma thoin." It means, "Kiss my ass."

I taught the phrase to Lewis, but rather than encourage him to use offensive language, I told him it meant, "You're very lovely." It was worth the price of the trip to hear the exchange with the waitress that evening.

"What's your name, Darling?"

"Colleen."

"Ah, Colleen, pog ma thoin," he said passionately.

EQUIPMENT

You are advised to eschew the "big hog" golf bags so often strapped on the back of American golf carts, because there's a great likelihood that bag will be strapped to your back in Scotland. While most courses have caddies, they look at you like you have a pox if you ask them to haul one of those "tour" bags.

A lightweight bag is essential, but that doesn't necessarily mean small. It should be large enough to hold your dirty underwear for the trip home.

Take two pairs of comfortable golf shoes, for you will be walking. No carts. You can wear the second pair while the first one dries out. And take a good rain suit. It's the outfit you'll be wearing in most of your photographs.

You'll be surprised how few balls you will need – a sleeve per round is usually adequate. The caddies rarely lose one, and there is very little water on the courses. Of course, the price you pay for the caddies' skill is often verbal abuse. Allow me two examples.

As we were tromping the heather looking for an errant shot one day, someone asked, "What kind of ball is it?"

The caddy answered quickly, "A brand-new one – never been properly hit!"

Another time a caddy pointed out a ball in the rough which he claimed was mine. "That can't be my ball," I said. "It looks far too old."

"But, sir," said the caddy, "it's been a long, long time since we started."

More about caddies later.

CLOTHING

You'll need a variety of clothing, from short sleeve golf shirts and sweater vests to turtleneck and warm sweaters. Remember that you'll be wallowing in the mother lode of woolen sweaters and will probably want to bring some home.

For ectomorphic golfers, silk long underwear provides warmth and comfort as well as a few winks in the locker room.

FOOD

It's hearty, good, stick-to-the-ribs fare. They have lots of cows in Ireland and sheep in Scotland, as well as fresh fish in both places, so all three make excellent choices.

Be sure you know what you're doing before you order the Scottish staple haggis. It was cooked in a sheep's stomach. And if you think you know everything that can be done to a pig to make it edible at breakfast, you'll learn a lot in Scotland.

The presentation of food is done with great élan in hotel restaurants. Usually, you are served by a team. The food is unveiled ceremoniously, and your expressions of delight are well received.

One member of our group had the best response of the trip when he was served chocolate mousse for dessert. It was grandly placed before him, three thick lines of dark brown chocolate mousse squeezed from a pastry bag onto a large, pristine white plate.

He looked at the waiter and said, "My compliments to the dog."

SPIRITS

The drinking kind, not the haunting kind. You have arrived in the motherland. Don't order a "Scotch" in Scotland, because it's all "Scotch" to them. They just call it whiskey.

You will recognize certain blends from the shelves in the U.S., but there is a plethora of single-malt whiskeys from little known regional distilleries throughout Scotland. Each is distinctive and worthy of debate among Scotch lovers in choosing *the* very best.

There are more brands to choose from than the A&P has cereal selections. I recommend taking home some of the obscure brands for gifts. Your friends will like it just because they can't get it at home; so what if it really tastes like creosote?

There also are wonderful regional beers, each with its own character and body. In gluttonous quantities, each can change your character and lead to out-of-body experiences.

INTERNATIONAL RELATIONS

There can be no friendlier, sweeter people on this earth than the Scots and Irish. You should be loathe to insult them. Read *The Ugly American* before you go, and don't invite Lewis Grizzard. Even friendly, sweet people have their limits, and we tested them trying to fly from Ireland to Scotland.

It was chaotic at the Shannon, Ireland, airport. We had played eighteen holes at Ballybunion and were hustling to make a flight to Edinburgh, Scotland, with a change of planes in Dublin. Murphy's law took over, and six of us were somehow dropped from the computer for the last leg of the flight.

By the time the problem was discovered in the Dublin airport, the flight was sold out except for two seats. Four of us would have to stay behind and find alternate transportation.

In the meantime, Lewis had made a startling discovery of his own – that the plane for the last leg of the flight was a commuter with propellors and an overhead wing. For a man who hates to fly in the best of circumstances, this was too much. He began preparing himself for the coming ordeal by taking on supplemental fuel. I think it was double screwdrivers. By the time the plane was ready for boarding, he was charming enough to be considered "tanked."

With reality staring him in his glazed eyes as he walked across the tarmac toward the waiting plane, Lewis made a quick decision to drive to Scotland (across the Irish Sea, we presume). He jumped into a fuel truck belonging to the Irish airline, Aer Lingus (which I think is Gaelic for "Fly My Tongue"), and started the truck's engine.

Forty-seven ramp attendants and two security guards with their hands on their weapons appeared from out of nowhere and convinced Lewis to get out of the truck. He was again aimed at the airplane, but before boarding, he decided to kick the tires to see if they were worthy. He reserved his verdict for a nun he encountered on the plane – "Pray for us, Sister," he said, "'cause this damn thing is going to crash!"

Meanwhile, back in the terminal where four of us waited for a plan to get to Scotland, Aer Lingus officials tried to placate us by saying there might be one additional seat to open up on the plane. Security personnel were about to remove one unruly passenger. We begged and pleaded with them not to remove that passenger – it could only be one person – that to do so might imperil the country. Lewis stayed on the plane.

The four stragglers, including your correspondent, were flown to London and then driven to a waiting train destined for Edinburgh. Overnight. Full of unwashed travelers from the Middle East and poor German students. With no stops for food, water, or beverage.

We arrived in Edinburgh, battered and bruised, just in time to catch a taxi to nearby Muirfield for our 10:30 A.M. tee time. Not even Jack Nicklaus misses a tee time at Muirfield.

Unfortunately, Aer Lingus had not, as they had promised, put our clubs and bags on the plane to Edinburgh. The result was that we had to tackle the legendary course with borrowed clubs and shoes.

As our weary group sat trying to piece together the proper ensemble, one member said, "I saw a man who had no shoes and I wept, until I saw a man who had no clubs."

CADDIES

Don't tee off without them. For one thing, the courses are not marked like the ones you're used to. There are no cart paths to guide you and, by definition, links courses are very natural and have many blind shots. The only disadvantage to a caddy is that they usually won't carry a cooler of iced-down beer like a cart will.

My advice is to listen to what the caddies tell you. They know the courses, and after a few holes they know you and your game. Nonetheless, I did manage to fool one for several holes at Gleneagles.

There is a pecking order of sorts when caddies choose the bags they want to carry; that order is based on seniority. I'm sure they look at the men to spot good tippers, the equipment to spot good golfers, and so forth.

This was my first encounter with a Scottish course. Combine that with jet lag, and I was as nervous as a man wearing trifocals at a strip joint. I hooked my first tee shot into a fairway bunker, got out OK and salvaged bogey. The next two holes produced solid double bogeys. My drive on the fourth tee again went off the fairway. As we walked toward the ball, my caddy, who had been extremely quiet, suddenly said with great scorn, "Normally when a man carries a *one* iron, he can play."

Caddies for afternoon rounds can be scarce, so it's best to book them for the entire day. Even that has its pitfalls, however. At St. Andrews we played The New Course at 8 A.M. and were scheduled to tee off on The Old Course at 3 P.M. Our caddies used the three hours between rounds to drink their profits in the local tavern. By the time we got on The Old Course, they were loop legged.

When I occasionally hit a good shot and held the pose at the top of my swing, my caddy would scream, "ICHIBAN! ICHIBAN!" Seems that he had been caddying for too many of the Japanese golfers who flock to St. Andrews with cameras in hand.

We picked up a lot of local color from these wonderful, surly ambassadors of mirth and golf history. Just their phrases alone are worth the price of admission:

- "Sir, hit it on a line directly between the paps in the distance." Say what? When he told me that "paps" means breasts, the terrain in the background became unmistakable.

- "Take it on a line just a wee bit right of the Scotsman lying on his back." This was a reference to a tall silo in the distance.

But they also can be demanding and critical:

- "Damn you, sir. I said *drrraw* it, not *hoook* it!"

- After I hit a particularly bad shot, my caddy turned to me and said, "And you call yourself a golfer."

- Another member of our group, trying to make conversation, said to his caddy, "I'll bet you caddy for some pretty bad golfers." The caddy replied, "Aye, laddie, I'm caddying for one now."

• Lewis's caddy at Nairn said to him, "You have a great short game, sir. Too bad it's off the tee." At the end of that round, Lewis tried to retaliate by saying, "You must be the worst caddy in the world." To which the caddy responded, "That, sir, would be too great a coincidence."

• Finally, after another string of bad holes, I tried to make light of the situation with my caddy. "You know," I said, "golf is a funny game." With an absolutely straight face, he said, "It's not supposed to be, sir."

A golfing trip to Scotland and Ireland is a dream you can live. There is nothing quite like it for those who love the game and its history. The charm of the Olde Sod may be oft imitated but never duplicated. And if anyone tells you otherwise, just tell 'em, "Pog ma thoin! ”

***

In Mexico, plush golf resorts have been built along the coasts. These are virtual leisure compounds, where the beautiful people eat, drink, swim, tan and play games. Just outside these compounds, however, is a very poor country with a low standard of living. People work hard for little money. The American dollar is strong, and everything is relatively cheap.

Several of us once spent four days playing courses around Ixtapa, Mexico. The green fee, for a plush facility, was about four dollars, and a cart for eighteen holes was less than that.

As we prepared to tee off the first day, a Mexican man in his late forties offered to serve as our forecaddy. Even though we had electric carts and didn't need a regular caddy, it was helpful to have someone along who knew the course and could help us find stray shots.

At the end of the round, Lupe had done an excellent job, so we each gave him ten dollars. His eyes bulged, and he asked excitedly if we were playing again the next day.

For four straight days, Lupe met us on the first tee and served as forecaddy, and each day we paid him ten dollars apiece. We knew that was a good deal of money to him, but we didn't fully realize how much.

I suppose we should have been tipped off when, on the third day, Lupe's wife met us at the turn with sandwiches she had prepared.

At the end of our round on the fourth day, Lupe again asked about the next day. When we told him we were leaving, that our vacation was over, he cried. The man wept because we were leaving. No, actually he wept because our American dollars were leaving.

***

The courses I played in Hawaii were mostly around mountains and volcanos. Of course, every one of them was plush, but that's no big deal in a land so fertile that tropical fruit trees grow out of what appears to be solid rock.

Many of the courses were on cliffs overlooking the ocean. And the wind blew steadily. And it was not a good idea to wear baggy shirts that could fill up with wind and become balloon-like. With you inside them.

Basically, there are two things that describe golf in Hawaii – long waits and pineapples.

***

I was looking forward to playing golf in Bermuda. I had seen photographs of the beautiful courses carved out of that tiny island. Pink sand. Clear blue water. It was like playing on a postcard.

I had arranged an invitation to play at the prestigious Mid-Ocean Club, one of the island's few private courses. Ve-dy British, photographs of scowling old men on the wall. Before I left the states, I had purchased a new pair of golfing shorts and a new shirt for the occasion.

Shorts are popular in Bermuda, especially Bermuda shorts. Makes sense, doesn't it? Men actually wear them to the office with knee socks, shirt, tie and coat. I couldn't help thinking of Little Lord Fauntleroy.

Anyway, I catch a taxi from my hotel to the golf course and am greeted there by a man who appears to be doorman.

"May I help you, sir?" he asks in a clipped British accent with his nose in the air.

"Yes, my good man," I counter. "I'm here to play golf."

"Not in those shorts, you're not," he says.

"What's wrong with these pants?" I ask, wondering who died and made this fellow king for the day.

"They're too short, sir. All you Americans think you can come over here and dress any way you like. Well, not on this course. This club has strict standards, sir, and your pants are definitely too short."

I argued for a good while longer, just out of principle. But when they started to call the U.S. Embassy, I figured maybe my pants were a little too short.

Not coincidentally, I was able to buy a pair that were the proper length – approximately one and a half inches longer than mine – in the pro shop. For a king's ransom.

If that scam were tried in the U.S., Ralph Nader would be on them like hair on a leg.

My round was most enjoyable, except for one embarrassing episode. I was still feeling a bit harassed when we teed off, and even when we reached the first green I was still thinking of ways to maim that uppity doorman.

Suddenly I was struck by the beauty of the green. The grass was so perfect, firm yet soft like carpet, with just a hint of blue in its deep green color.

"This green is beautiful," I said to my host. "Is it bent grass?"

He looked at me without a smile and said, "No, Bermuda."

More Stories About Those Catty Caddies

Near the end of a particularly trying round of golf, during which the golfer had hit numerous fat shots, he said in frustration to his caddy, "I'd move heaven and earth to break a hundred on this course."

"Try heaven," said the caddy. "You've already moved most of the earth."

***

Standing on the tee of a relatively long par three, the confident golfer said to his caddy, "Looks like a four-wood and a putt to me." The caddy handed him the four-wood, which he topped about fifteen yards off the front of the tee. Immediately the caddy handed him his putter and said, "And now for one hell of a putt."

***

The golfer sliced his drive deep into the gorse, and the diligent caddy followed him in. After several minutes, they found the ball under a thick branch.

"Do you know what kind of shot I'll need here?" asked the golfer.

"Yes, sir," answered the caddy. And he pulled a hip flask from his back pocket.

***

"Caddy, why do you keep looking at your watch?" asked the curious golfer.

"It's not a watch, sir. It's a compass."

***

For most of the round the golfer had argued with his caddy about club selection, but the caddy always prevailed. Finally on the seventeenth hole, a 185-yard par three into the wind, the caddy handed the golfer a four-wood and the golfer balked.

"I think it's a three-iron," said the golfer.

"No, sir, it's a four-wood," said the caddy.

"Nope, it's definitely the three-iron."

So the golfer set up, took the three-iron back slowly, and struck the ball perfectly. It tore through the wind, hit softly on the front of the green, and rolled up two feet short of the pin.

"See," said the caddy. "I told you it wasn't enough club."

***

The golfer tried three straight times to hit the ball over the inlet of water between him and the green, but each time the ball splashed into the drink. In utter frustration, the golfer said, "Caddy, take my clubs on in. I'm going to jump in the water and drown myself."

"I doubt that, sir. You couldn't keep your head down long enough to drown."

***

The man came in from a long afternoon of golf. His wife met him at the door with a kiss. A few minutes later their son came in looking tired and weary.

"Where's he been?" asked the father.

"He's been caddying for you all afternoon," said his wife.

"No wonder that kid looked so familiar."

You Probably Don't Remember Me, But...

A couple of years ago, I was invited to play in that elegant golf tournament known simply as The Crosby. It is whatever happened to the Bing Crosby tournament in California that drew the stars and the game's top players for so many years.

The late crooner had indicated that if there came a time that less than fifty percent of the proceeds of his tournament were going to charity, it should be halted, moved or somehow altered to return to its roots as an event held primarily to help the less fortunate.

The demands for a large purse for the pros finally did deplete the charitable funds, and Crosby's widow, Kathryn, packed the whole thing up and moved it to Burmuda Run Country Club in Winston-Salem, North Carolina. The tournament raises approximately one million dollars for charity each year.

It was an incredible experience. For four days I played between the ropes, just like the stars of the PGA.

The Saturday crowd was estimated at over twenty thousand. I, an eleven-handicapper who shouldn't be that low, hit a screaming three-iron twelve feet from the pin on the watery seventeenth hole in front of five thousand people.

When I arrived at the green to applause just like at the Masters, I did my best Jack Nicklaus smile and waved.

I missed the putt, but I made par and it was bigger than the time in high school when I hit the pop fly that rolled into the weeds by the concession stand, and before the ball was found, I was around the bases for the winning run.

I also topped a few off the tee, left one in the trap on eighteen, and lost my players badge and was nearly thrown off the course by a security guard, who said with a sneer, "You don't look like no golfer." But I didn't hurt anybody.

I also got to meet a lot of famous people. Bob Hope was there. I shook his hand. I met Dale Robertson (who played in *The Tales of Wells Fargo*), McClean Stevenson, Claude Akins, Efrem Zimbalist, Jr., football's Dick (Night Train) Lane and Jim McMahon, the goofy quarterback.

I also played a round with Jim Palmer as my partner. Jim Palmer is the former pitcher for the Baltimore Orioles who now shows up on billboards wearing nothing but his Jockey underwear.

Women love Jim Palmer.

"You're absolutely gorgeous," one woman said to him at the sixth hole.

"Jim Palmer!" exclaimed another at the tenth. "I didn't recognize you with your clothes on."

It went on like that all day and I, quite frankly, got a little tired of it. It was difficult to putt with a large group of women offering up various mating calls.

Finally, however, one woman did say to me, "Lewis, what kind of underwear do you have on?"

"Not any," I replied, leaving her eating the dust of my golf cart.

* * *

Another time I played in singer Larry Gatlin's tournament, which benefits the Muscular Dystrophy Association. In my group was a monstrous professional football player named Glen Titsensor. He was a Dallas Cowboy at the time.

On one hole Titsensor swung a four-iron so hard that the head of the club came off the shaft and traveled farther from the tee than my ball had.

"I used to hit the ball like that before my operation," I said to Mr. Cowboy.

"What did you have?" he replied. "A muscle-ectomy?"

I didn't laugh because I didn't think it was that funny. But one more smart aleck remark from this palooka, I thought to myself, and I'm not going to send him a Christmas card next year.

But that's not the point of this story. The point is that on the sixth hole we were off the edge of the fairway, searching for a men's room, when someone yelled, "Snake!"

As I have explained earlier, I am afraid of snakes. Make that terrified. Even more afraid than I am of obnoxious Dallas Cowboys. I don't even look at pictures of snakes in magazines.

Mr. Cowboy, of course, was not at all afraid of the snake. He picked it up by the tail and said, "It's just a little garter snake."

I disagreed with his identification. It looked a lot like the dreaded copper-headed water rattler to me. They all do.

Mr. Cowboy just laughed, put the snake down on the ground, and jiggled his size-sixteen tennis shoe at it. The snake tried several times to bite the shoe. Mr. Cowboy laughed. I didn't need the men's room anymore. The snake slithered off into the bushes.

A couple of minutes later, when order was restored, I dubbed my shot off into the bushes where the snake had gone. I left it there for the weeds and the ages.

One fact of life I know for sure: Never give a snake that has just been embarrassed by a Dallas Cowboy the chance to get even on somebody with a physique that strongly resembles a four-iron.

***

Probably the highlight of my pro-am career came before the 1987 Heritage Classic at the Harbour Town Golf Links at Hilton Head, South Carolina.

The week before, Australian golfing great Greg Norman had lost the Masters golf tournament in overtime when Larry Mize chipped in from the next county. Before he could even recover, Norman suffered another traumatic experience at the Heritage – he drew me as one of his partners in the pro-am.

I figured that after losing the Masters, Norman would be justifiably quiet and maybe even pout a little. But not so. He signed about three thousand autographs and posed for at least that many pictures during our round.

As I watched him smile his way through all that, I thought of a young sportswriter who had tried to interview baseball's Darryl Strawberry of the Mets during spring training. The kid had asked Strawberry a simple question.

"Out of my face" is how Strawberry had answered him.

Norman had a bad round in the pro-am; he shot five over par.

I lost control of my game and birdied the fifth hole. On No. 6, I chipped in from off the green for another birdie.

"I've seen that shot before," said Norman, referring to Mize's winning chip against him in Augusta. "And it was going the same speed," he added, referring to the fact that both Mize's shot and my shot would still be rolling had they not gone into the hole.

***

I've played golf with a number of golf's best, as a matter of fact. Want a list? Okay.

- TOM WATSON: Nice person. Told me I wasn't turning my hips.

- PAUL AZINGER: Hates sportswriters. I didn't mention I used to be one.

- ANDY BEAN: Could have been a linebacker.

• HALE IRWIN: At the Federal Express Pro-Am in Memphis. It was 200 degrees. He didn't sweat.

• CHI CHI RODRIGUEZ: I told a joke to the gallery. They laughed. He said, "I'm the comedian here."

• KEITH CLEARWATER: My girlfriend wanted to marry him.

• GEORGE ARCHER: At the Doral Pro-Am. Never spoke.

• ARNOLD PALMER: Yes, I played eighteen holes with Arnold Palmer at Bay Hill in Orlando. Arnold Palmer praised my good shots, didn't say anthing about my bad ones, made an eagle on Bay Hill's par-five sixteenth and got just as excited as he did when he was winning everything in sight. I made a three on a hole he made four on and we were playing from the same tees. Arnold Palmer has a dog named "Riley," hit a 270-yard three-wood, his secretary brought him a portable phone on the course so he could return his calls, and he's in his sixties and looks about forty-five.

I have eaten dinner with two presidents, sang on stage with Larry Gatlin, shook hands with Bob Hope, been to New York City several times and Paris once, kissed the best-looking cheerleader in the history of the Atlanta Falcons square in the mouth and have played golf with Arnold Palmer. My life is complete.

Gatewood Dooper At The Masters

As one who earned his rent money on the working side of the press for a number of years, I had the opportunity to cover a lot of professional golf tournaments.

I was in Augusta when Roberto DeVecenzio signed an erroneous score card. I was there years later when an aging Jack Nicklaus roared one more time. I was at the U.S. Open when Fuzzy Zeller almost pulled it off; that's what America needed, I wrote – a U.S. Open champion named Fuzzy.

Each of the tournaments I covered was different, each with its own brand of excitement and pageantry. But two things were always the same, no matter where you were. One, the sandwiches always tasted like they had been made the day before, because they had. And two, the post-round interviews always sounded the same.

You may have seen one or two of these interviews if you watch a lot of ESPN. After a good round, a golfer is invited into the press area and asked to go over his round, shot by shot.

Once at a U.S. Open I listened as Ben Crenshaw went over his round, which had momentarily tied him for the lead. In the middle of his summary, he said, "On eleven, I hit a four-wood to the corner, had about 175 yards to the green, and hit an eight-iron to about twelve feet. Then I missed the . . ."

"Whoa, just a minute!" I said, surprising even myself. "You hit an eight-iron how far?" I mean, he's a little fellow.

"About 175 yards," said Crenshaw matter-of-factly. Seeing the bewilderment on my face, he added, "It was downhill."

Downhill, molehill. I don't think I could hit an eight-iron 175 yards with Hurricane Hugo behind me.

But most of the guys on the PGA tour are so good, and so strong, that listening to them recount their rounds has as much meaning to me as listening to someone explain mathematical equations.

I have this recurring fantasy about listening to a different kind of golfer go over his round at the Masters. I know what Nicklaus did. He hit a drive down the middle four thousand yards, hit a wedge to the stick and tapped it in with his middle finger. And on sixteen, he walked across the water to the green after holing his tee shot. That's everyday stuff.

I want them to bring in Gatewood Dooper from the Clubfoot Links in Oshkosh, who got into the tournament by some strange quirk of Masters eligibility fate and then played like a goat with muscular dystrophy.

Let me hear *him* go over his round with the world's press assembled. Here is Gatewood Dooper describing his 107, the worst round in Masters history:

"On the very first tee, I wet my pants. That's a two-stroke penalty and very embarrassing. I was hitting three on my opening drive. It landed in a trap. I wound up with a nine. My wife went back to the car.

"On No. 2, I went into the trap again. The one behind No. 3 green. I managed to save double bogey. My sponsor made an obscene gesture and went looking for my wife.

"On three, four and five, I had bogeys. My caddy agreed to stay for one more hole. I triple-bogeyed No. 6 and he went back to my car, too. To slice my tires.

"At seven, I hit a spectator. I had to. He came at me with a rock.

"I made the turn at seventeen-over. Before I teed off on ten, the tournament committee asked me to withdraw, my wife came back to the course and asked me for a divorce, and my sponsor stripped his company's name off my bag and hat.

"I fell into the lake on No. 12. One of the marshals pushed me. My drive went into the crowd lining the fairway at thirteen. I had to take another penalty. They hid my ball.

"No. 14 and No. 15 were both disasters. At sixteen, they threw beer at me. At seventeen, I twisted my ankle. My playing partner tripped me. At eighteen, they sang 'Turkey in the Straw' while I tried to hit out of the rough.

"After I finally putted out, they put my card in the paper shredder and I had to hightail it to the locker room. The tournament committee had ordered sniper fire from the roof of Ike and Mamie's cottage."

Tough luck, Gatewood, but hang in there. There's more of us who understand your round than understand a 175-yard eight-iron.

A Tale Of Two Lifestyles

Here is a twist on an oft-told story. I'm sure we've all been here at one time or another.

All his life, the dignified State Supreme Court Justice from South Carolina had dreamed of playing a round of golf at that Southern holy of golf holies, the Augusta National. But he had never met a member or been able to wrangle an invitation from someone who did. While passing through Augusta one day, he couldn't resist the urge to at least drive by and gaze at the course – or actually at the stately gates which lead to it.

Though he knew better, the primal pull led him to drive up to the gatekeeper. As the frowning man approached, the Judge rolled down his window and said, "I am Judge Poteet from Charleston, and I'm in town on business. Would it be possible for me to just drive down Magnolia Lane once?" →

"Sorry," replied the eloquent guardian.

As he was turning around to leave, another car was turning in to the driveway. Losing all sixty-three years of dignity, he rolled down his window and stuck his head out as a signal for the driver to stop. He began talking fast.

"Are you a member of this marvelous club?" he prayed aloud.

"Of course," came the unamused reply.

Pressing forward, he continued, "Sir, I am Judge Poteet of Charleston, South Carolina, and I have been a lifelong devotee of golf. Although I have attended the Masters golf tournament for the last thirty-seven years, I have never had the privilege of playing this course. My life will not be complete until I've struck a golf ball inside these walls. Is there any way, sir, that you could help me?"

"Let's get out of the driveway," the member answered, and he gestured for the highly excited judge to follow him in.

He couldn't believe it. He was actually driving his car down the historic, picturesque, magnolia-shrouded lane leading toward the most beautiful and restricted golf club in the world. Could this be happening?

When they got to the parking lot, he jumped out of his car and rushed over to the member.

"I appreciate your taking a moment to →

consider my request, sir. I know this is completely out of order, but I would consider the opportunity to play here the crowning achievement of my life – and a great personal favor."

The member gave the judge a long look, shut his car door and asked, "Handicap?"

"Eleven, sir, though during my younger years I was a scratch golfer."

"Education?"

"Duke, undergrad, Harvard Law School – magna cum laude."

"Athletics?"

"Duke golf team. Was medalist on the '58 ACC champion team that beat Palmer's Wake Forest team in a playoff. Also lettered in all four sports in high school."

"Military?"

"Army intelligence, Korea. Purple heart and Bronze Star."

"Community involvement?"

"State coordinator for American Heart Association, '72 through '79. Chamber of Commerce, Lions' Club, church deacon."

"Club membership?"

"Charleston Country Club, Melrose, Pinehurst."

The member pondered briefly, then nodded to the young man from the club who had walked out to see if his assistance was needed, and said, "Let him hit a bucket of balls."

Divorce: An American Golf Tragedy

The most difficult tickets to obtain in all of sport are those which allow the holder to walk upon the hallowed grounds of Augusta National Golf Club during the annual Masters Tournament.

There are no sales to the general public. Those who have tickets either inherited them or got on the list for the privilege of buying them years ago.

What follows is a warning to those men . . . and maybe a demonic tip for their women.

Jack, an acquaintance, first began buying tickets twenty-three years ago.

"They were just fifteen dollars back then," he said, "but they went up to seventy."

Jack used to go to the tournament each year with three friends, Bill, Gene and Sid.

"We would leave home at six in the morning," he recalled. "There was a little beer store on the way. We'd wait at the door with the pulpwood workers until the guy came to open up. We had some great times and saw some great golf. But then my wife got to be a big problem for me and my Masters tickets."

"I heard that," I said.

"She just hated for me to have a good time," Jack went on. "She didn't like me going to the Masters or playing golf or fishing or running with my buddies. I was on a leash. I was a salesman and my territory was the Southeast. On Friday afternoons on my way home, I enjoyed stopping by the Elks Club and having a few beers with my buddies."

"And your wife didn't like that?"

"Of course not. She'd start yelling at me the minute I got home: 'Jack, you stopped by the Elks Club, didn't you? How many beers did you have?'

"I always said two. I usually had twenty-seven. She'd say, 'Why do you always say two?' and I'd say, 'What difference does it make what I tell you? You don't believe anything I say anyway.' One day she got so mad at me she went to my closet and took out all my clothes, and then she got my golf clubs and went out on the deck and covered them with charcoal lighter and set them on fire."

"But what about the Masters tickets, Jack?"

"Several years ago," he continued, "they cut my allotment down. I used to get four but they cut me to two. Well, that ended our group going to the tournament, and by this time my wife had gotten herself a job at the courthouse, and she started thinking she was pretty high and mighty and she wanted to be seen in all the right places. So she began going to the Masters with me just to be seen, but she never wanted to stay over an hour.

"One thing led to another and we finally got a divorce. I was so sick and tired of everything I wanted it to be over as fast as possible.

"So when the lawyers came to me, I told them my wife could have everything, the house included. I signed the papers without really looking at them. And do you know what she had put in those papers?"

"Don't tell me."

"Yep. She had them put in that she got my two Masters tickets. And she doesn't even like golf. She did it out of spite."

"That's one of the saddest stories I've ever heard," I said. "To have once had Masters tickets and then to have lost them to an ex-wife. Have you ever tried to get them back from her?"

"I'm afraid to," said Jack. "A woman who'll take your Masters tickets would kill you if she got half the chance."

I heard that, too.

President Dwight D. Eisenhower was an avid golfer with a good sense of humor, and one of his favorite golf jokes was told by Tennessee Ernie Ford, also a golf fan. Anytime the two were together, Eisenhower urged Ford to tell this joke:

One spring day the Lord and Moses were sitting in Heaven looking down at the Earth when their eyes fell upon the beautiful Augusta National Golf Course. There was no one on the course, and the two had the same idea at the same time: "It's so beautiful, why don't we drop down and just play the back nine."

When they came to the sixteenth hole, the picturesque par three over water, the Lord said, "I think I'm going to hit a seven-iron."

Moses thought for a moment and then said, "I'm not sure that's enough. I think you should hit a six-iron."

"No," said the Lord, "I'm going to hit the seven. That's what Arnold Palmer hits, so that's what I'm going to hit."

So the Lord hit the seven-iron, but it came up about six yards short and landed in the water. Without a word, Moses parted the water, walked out and retrieved the Lord's ball. →

"Maybe now you'll hit the six-iron," said Moses.

"No," answered the Lord, "I'm going to hit the seven-iron again. If Palmer can do it, so can I."

"Well," said Moses, "if you hit it in the water again, I'm not going after it this time."

Sure enough, the Lord hit a seven-iron again, and again it fell short into the water. The Lord lay his club down and walked across the water to fetch his ball.

Just at that time, another foursome came up from behind them. One of the men spotted the Lord walking on the water and said to Moses, "Who does that guy think he is, Jesus Christ?"

"He *is* Jesus Christ. He thinks he's Arnold Palmer!" said Moses.

***

The great Sam Snead, known in some circles for his biting sarcasm as much as for his golf, was conducting a clinic at a chic club. A woman raised her hand and asked, "Mr. Snead, how do you make a three-iron back up?"

Snead thought for a moment and then asked, "M'am, how far do you hit a three-iron?"

"About 150 yards," answered the woman.

"Then why in the hell would you want to back it up?" said Snead.

After being away from home for three months trying to make it on the European tour, the golf pro was finally back in bed with his wife, hoping to make up for lost time. Later in the evening when they were asleep, there was a loud knock at the door, and they both sat up straight.

"My god, that must be your husband!" exclaimed the golf pro.

"No, it can't be," said his wife. "He's in Europe playing golf."

***

Bob stood over his tee shot on the eighteenth hole for what seemed like forever. He'd waggle, look down, look up, waggle, look down, look up, but would never start his backswing. Finally David, his playing partner, asked, "Why on earth are you taking so long on this shot?"

"My wife is up there watching me from the clubhouse, and I want to make this shot a good one," said Bob.

"Good Lord," said David, "you ain't got a chance of hitting her from here."

Quayle Is Being Kicked In The Putt

As soon as George Bush nominated Dan Quayle to be his running mate, the young senator started taking a licking from the press. Even after two years as vice president of the United States, he is better known as a joke writer than a politician.

I have, until now, tried to be supportive of Vice President Quayle, because he reminds me of an old hound dog of mine who used to chase cars. (He finally caught one.) But a recent revelation about the vice president has undermined my confidence in him.

An article in *Sports Illustrated* cited Quayle's fondness for golf. He has, in fact, been referred to as "Florida's third senator," because of all the time he spends in that golfing paradise. But that's not the big deal.

The article also quoted Randy Reifers, who was a golfing teammate of Quayle's at DePauw University. When asked to describe Vice President Quayle's game, Reifers, who lives in Dublin, Ohio, said: "Quayle still can't beat me. He never could putt."

As everyone who plays golf knows, putting – the actual stroking of the ball into the hole – is where the head gets involved in the game more than at any other time.

Putting is a touch. Putting is confidence. Putting is a test of the nerves.

The pro players know the axiom "Drive for show, putt for dough." Everybody on the pro tour is a marvelous golfer. But those who win tournaments and the big bucks are the ones who can sink a four-foot, downhill birdie putt on national television with a couple hundred big ones on the line.

My point is simply this: Putting is not only a true test of one's nerves; it's also a true test of one's character.

People who can't putt are lily-livered chokers who eventually commit suicide or go insane and take up bowling.

I know this to be true, because I, as much as I hate to admit it, am a terrible putter.

I can make a putt for double-bogey occasionally because there is very little pressure involved in it. But give me a short putt for par or birdie and . . . I perspire heavily. My mouth becomes exceedingly dry. I begin to breathe laboriously. My pupils dilate. My hands shake.

And I miss the blankety-blank putt.

Another couple of bad putting years and I'll have to decide whether or not it's worth going on living if I have to become a bowler.

My question here is, Are we safe with a man who can't putt only a heartbeat away from the Presidency?

Doesn't this revelation prove that Vice President Quayle, like myself, can't take the heat? Can't make the big one when he has to?

I realize many Americans feel the press has been very harsh on Quayle, but I cannot stand idly by and not make the American public aware of this flaw in the vice president.

When I think of a national leader, I think of someone who never leaves a putt short, who firms a ball into the hole with a smooth, steady stroke despite any pressure.

I say Ben Crenshaw for vice president in '92!

A man called the pro shop to get a tee time for the afternoon.

"I'm sorry, sir," said the pro, "but we're all filled up."

"Wait a minute," countered the man. "If Dan Quayle called and said he wanted a tee time this afternoon, could you get him on?"

"Well, of course we could, sir."

"Well, fine. I happen to know that the Vice President is out of the country today, so I'll take his tee time."

Two guys from New Jersey are playing golf together, both using Titleist DT2 balls. On a long par four, they both hit great drives right down the middle. When they get to the balls, however, one of them has a very bad lie while the other is sitting up perfectly.

"I'm sure this is my ball," says Vinnie, standing over the good lie.

"No, you're wrong," says Harvey. "That's definitely my ball."

The two argue about whose ball is which for ten minutes. Finally they decide to go get the pro and let him settle the argument.

When the pro returns, he says, "Well, guys, I think I can settle this for you pretty quick. Who's playing the yellow ball?"

***

"If I died, would you remarry?" asked the wife.

"Probably so," answered the husband.

"And would your new wife take my place as your golfing partner?" she asked, a bit hurt.

"Probably so," answered the husband.

"And would you give her my new golf clubs?" she asked indignantly.

"Of course not," said the husband. "She's left-handed."

Kiss My Ace, It Really Went In

On a glorious November day in 1989, I made a hole-in-one on the St. Simons, Georgia, Island Club course.

Honest, I did. This isn't one of those make-believe things I sometimes write. I mean that I hit a golf ball on a par three and it went into the hole for a "1."

Do you know the thrill of writing a "1" on a golf scorecard next to your name?

I've had my thrills in sports before. Playing for dear old Newnan High back in '63, I hit a jump shot at the buzzer to defeat the top-seeded team in the region tournament. That got my name and picture in the paper. (I wanted a kiss from a certain red-headed cheerleader, but she remarked how she detested kissing anyone covered in sweat.)

I also pitched a no-hitter in Pony League, finished second in a tennis tournament, hit a hard-way six on a crap table in Vegas, made back-to-back net eagles playing with Greg Norman in a pro-am golf tournament in

Hilton Head, and once had dinner with the girl who used to say, "Take it off. Take it *all* off," in the old shaving-cream commercials.

(I realize having dinner with a girl who made a shaving-cream commercial has nothing to do with sports, but she made the commercial with Joe Namath, so there.)

But none of that compares with my hole-in-one.

Get the picture:

I'm on the par three, twelfth hole at the lovely Island Club in coastal Georgia. I admit No. 12 isn't that long a hole, but I didn't design the course, so it's not my fault.

The hole is 128 yards over a small pond.

It was Saturday morning, November 4. I was playing in a threesome, comprised of myself, Tim Jarvis and Mike Matthews, two players of lesser talent with whom I often hang out.

It was a lovely morning, having warmed to the low seventies as I approached the tee. I was wearing an orange golf shirt, a pair of Duckhead khaki slacks and my black and white golf shoes, the ones my dogs have not chewed up yet.

I was first on the tee.

"What are you going to hit?" asked Matthews.

"None of your business," I said. We were playing for a lot of money.

OK, so we weren't playing for a lot of money, but you never tell your opponent what club you are hitting.

"Tell us," said Jarvis, "or we'll tell everybody how you move the ball in the rough when nobody is looking."

"Nine-iron," I said.

The green sloped to the right. I said to myself, "Keep the ball to the left of the hole."

(Actually, I said, "Please, God, let me get this thing over the water.")

I hit a high, arching shot. The ball cut through the still morning air, a white missile against the azure sky. (That's the way Dan Jenkins or Herbert Warren Wind would have described it.)

The ball hit eight feet left of the pin. It hopped once. It hopped again. It was rolling directly toward the hole.

An eternity passed.

It has a chance to go in, I thought. But that's not going to happen, of course, because I'm terribly unlucky and I've done some lousy things in my life and I don't deserve for it to go into the hole.

It went into the hole.

A "1."

It was a joyous moment when my first hole-in-one fell snugly into the hole. But the best moment came at the next tee, the par-four thirteenth.

For any non-golfers, the person with the lowest score on the previous hole gets to hit first on the next hole. I strode to the tee with my driver, teed up my ball and then said to my opponents, "I think I'm up, but did anybody have a zero?"

Jarvis and Matthews were good friends, and I shall miss them.

Wayne, who was seventy-two years old, still loved to play golf, but his eyesight had become so poor that he couldn't follow the flight of his ball anymore. He was about to give up the game when the club pro suggested a solution. "Why don't you take old Harvey with you when you play?"

"Harvey? He's eighty years old and can't even play," said Wayne.

"Yeah, but his eyesight is perfect, and he could watch your ball for you."

Wayne decided to give it a try. At least it was better than giving up the game he so loved. The next day Wayne and Harvey stood on the first tee. Wayne smacked his drive squarely. He turned to Harvey and said, "Did you see it?"

"Yep," said Harvey, "sure did."

"So where is it?" asked Wayne.

"I forget," said Harvey.

***

"Kathy, if you don't stop nagging me," said the golfer to his wife, "you'll drive me out of my mind."

"That wouldn't be a drive. It would be more like a gimme putt."

The Men's Grill: The Final Frontier

As you may have noticed while reading through this book, golf is full of rituals – getting up the bet, talking in clichés, razing the guy who's playing poorly. But no ritual is as sacred as that of the Nineteenth Hole.

This is when, at the end of a round, the participants adjourn to the men's grill to enjoy a cold drink, to settle the bet, and to replay the highlights and lowlights of the just completed round.

In a men's grill, a man can be himself. He is surrounded only by his own kind, by golfers and gin players and drinkers, and a strong camaraderie develops over time.

Recently, however, at one of the clubs where I belong, this sanctuary was challenged. Female members of the opposite sex petitioned the club's membership in an attempt to be admitted to the men's grill.

An emergency meeting of the men's grill gang was called to address this crisis. Due to the seriousness of the issue, I feel it is my duty to release the confidential transcript of that meeting so that other men's grills, should they be confronted by the same challenge, may be better suited to deal with it. (Didn't Daniel Ellsberg go to jail for something like this?)

"This meeting of the Potookie Golf and Country Club's Men's Grill and Grab-ass Association will now come to order . . . or close to it," announced Shorty Milsaps, president of the group.

The boys gunned down the last swallows of their beers and gave Shorty their attention.

"Men," Shorty began, "as most of you know, a bunch of pinheaded women's libbers have petitioned the membership of this fine club to be admitted to the men's grill. They want to sit down here amongst us and ruin our good times. And it's my job to level with you and tell you that they got a chance to win this one."

"Are you serious, Shorty?" asked Cooter Carnes.

"As serious as your mother-in-law's drawers," replied Shorty.

There was much murmuring and cursing, and finally Gilbert Harskins said, "We got to fight this, men. This is the last place we got. You can't get away from women at work no more. They are on television giving the news. They are even driving buses and attending the Rotary Club. I wouldn't be surprised to see one playin' outfield for the Pirates before it's over."

"Hell," said Marvin Coddlemeyer, "if we get women in here, we going to have to change a lot of things."

"Like what?" asked Gilbert Harskins.

"Well, for one thing, we won't be able to spit on the floor or have the weekly belchin' contest. Women don't go in for spittin' on the floor or belchin'. We'll also have to quit telling nasty jokes, and Leon Caldwell won't be able to do that funny thing where he paints eyes on his belly and uses his navel for a mouth and pantomimes, 'She Was Just a Stableman's Daughter, But All the Horsemen Knew Her.'"

"That'd be a shame," said Cooter Carnes.

"I'll tell you what else," said Marvin Coddlemeyer. "Women will want to have congealed salad and celery sticks in here 'stead of Vienna sausages and beef jerky. And I guarantee you it won't be a month before they'll be sittin' around here drinkin' white wine and talkin' about their hair stylists."

"Marvin's right," said Cooter Carnes. "A man's just got to have a place he can go now and then and just be himself and say what he wants to and scratch where it itches. Dammit, Leon, quit spittin' on my shoes."

Curtis Knowles hadn't said a word during the entire discussion. Curtis had been married four times – once to a lady lawyer – and was held as an expert on females.

"Boys," he said, "if a woman can sit here with us and listen to all the bull and put up with chewin', spittin', belchin', cussin', and Leon Caldwell's navel, I say she's what I've been lookin' for all my life and hadn't been able to find. A woman who would put up with a man just bein' himself."

A hush fell over the crowd.

"I move we put an ad in the paper," said Cooter Carnes. "I'd like to meet a woman like that myself."

"Why don't you play golf with Dick anymore?" the inquiring wife asked her husband. "You two used to have a regular game."

"Well," said the husband, "would you play golf with a man who talks during your backswing, moves his ball around in the rough, forgets to take penalty shots, and never pays his bets when he loses?"

"Certainly not," said the wife.

"Well, Dick won't either."

***

George and his wife were playing a round of golf together when he sliced a drive behind a barn adjacent to the course. When they found his ball, his wife noticed that doors on both ends of the barn were open and suggested that George try to play through the opening. He took a mighty swing and hit the ball squarely. Unfortunately, it hit the frame of the door squarely and ricocheted backwards, striking his wife right between the eyes and killing her instantly.

About a year later George was playing the same hole with a friend and sliced his drive behind the barn again. When he started to pick up the ball and take a penalty shot, he friend said, "Hey, the doors on both ends of the barn are open. Why don't you just play through there?"

"Oh, no," said George. "Last time I tried that I made triple bogey."

When Did You Get That Hitch In Your Swing?

This is a chapter about all the other things about golf I couldn't figure out where to put into another chapter.

Like gamesmanship. Gamesmanship is a way to cheat in golf without breaking any of golf's 417,000 rules. It's a mental thing, a way to get inside your opponent's head and remember that ninety percent of golf is half mental, which Old Tom Morris said one day after a round at Old Prestwick in Scotland as he was sipping some Very Old Scotch in a country where everything is old.

There are many ways to play mind games in golf.

There's the old "When did you get that hitch in your swing?" ruse. Your opponent is two-over after fourteen holes. He nails one down the middle on fifteen. You say, "Great drive, Earl, but when did you get that hitch in your swing?"

Earl's mind says to Earl, "Hitch. What hitch? I don't have a hitch. But if I don't have a hitch, why did he mention it? Could it be the old 'When did you get that hitch in your swing?' ruse? It could be. But maybe it isn't. Maybe I do have a hitch in my swing. When did I get it? Sitting on a dirty commode stool in a truck stop?"

The very next time Earl swings he will have his mind on the hitch thing, and he'll hit the ball sideways. Your mind says to you, "You devil, you."

Then there's the old, "Didn't I see your wife in Goalby's the other night?" trick. Goalby's is a pick-up bar and your opponent's wife has never been there, but the seed has been planted. Your opponent will forget all about his golf game after that and concern himself with finding either a good lawyer or a large gun.

If your opponent hits his ball into the deep rough, golf etiquette requires that you help look for the lost ball; however, it doesn't require you to look all that hard.

Nonetheless, great skill is required to act earnest and concerned on the outside while howling on the inside. The proper dialogue is, "I just don't understand; it wasn't hit *that* bad"; or, "I'm sure it's around here somewhere"; or, "Maybe a squirrel ate it."

Gamesmanship sometimes takes on the appearance of courtesy. Dangerous animals live on some golf courses. You can use this fact to your advantage, as well. Say your opponent has you down three-and-none and is already talking about how much fun he'll have driving your car. Suddenly he duck hooks one deep into the woods.

If he doesn't find it, he must go back and retee the ball and you will win the hole. It becomes necessary, then, to insure that he doesn't find his original shot.

You might say, "Be careful in there, Grover. The pro said he saw a snake as big as his arm in there last week." This will do two things. It will cut down on how deeply Grover goes into the woods to look for his ball, and if he does find it and can hit it, the notion a snake as big as the pro's arm is somewhere around him will ensure a quick swing and perhaps he won't be able to get the ball back to the fairway.

There are other animals that live in the woods on golf courses besides snakes. You can say to your opponent, "Herb Gaines said he saw a wild pig in there last week."

Or, "Phil Daniels was in these very same woods Sunday and a big black dog walked up to him and bit him. He'll be taking rabies shots for a month."

Or, "Did you hear the gorilla got loose from the circus last week?" or, "Watch out for wooleyboogers in there."

Your opponent will ask, "What's a wooleybooger?"

You answer, "I don't know, but they say the sons of bitches have three eyes and carry machetes."

You devil, you.

Then there's what's down in the lagoon on coastal golf courses.

Alligators:

- "I think you stopped just short of the hazard, Al, but be careful because there's a lot of alligators in this lagoon."

- "Walter Sommers hit his ball in the same place you did, over near the lagoon, and just as he was about to hit it, an alligator the size of a Greyhound bus swam up on the bank. Walter never heard it. I'd have gone to his funeral today if I hadn't already scheduled this game. They never did find his other leg, by the way."

• "I think your shot stayed up. It's just on the edge of the lagoon. Did you know alligators can run sixty miles an hour?"

I was in a foursome at Melrose once, and my partner went over the green on the par five third hole. His ball stopped just short of the lagoon. He had a shot, but his ball had landed three feet from an alligator lying on the bank getting a bit of sun.

My partner said, "There's an alligator near my ball. I'm going to drop in over there."

One of our opponents said, "It will cost you a shot. You're in the hazard."

Not allowing an opponent an alligator drop is very mean-spirited. What my partner did was declare himself in his pocket and left the ball next to the alligator. Several days later, he went over to our opponent's house and set fire to his car.

Here are some other things you can casually remark to an opponent to ensure his mind will turn to mush:

• "If you took a little bigger swing, you really could get out there on your drive."

• "I called the office at the turn. The market's down thirty points."

• "Have you had your house checked for radon yet?"

• "You really do keep your left arm straight, don't you?"

• "There's an out of bounds on the left. Don't hit it over there."

• "You mean I'm past you? I just hit a three-wood."

• "Did you hear that Alice Farnsworthy has herpes? You used to date her, didn't you?"

And, in conclusion, the following:

• The hardest course I've ever played. Bay Hill, Orlando, from the tips, 7,100 yards, with Arnold Palmer. Into the wind. I was so nervous my caddy's hands were shaking. I shot the national deficit.

• The best recent innovation in golf: Carts with two container holders on each side. There's a place for your can AND your cup of ice. Before, you either had to put your can or your cup of ice on the floorboard of the cart and it would spill all over your new Foot-joys three seconds later.

• My favorite golf clichés: "Hit it, Alice" or, "Does your husband play golf, too?" on a putt left short. And, "Good roll," which everybody says when you miss a putt.

• The most certain thing in golf: "Good rolls" never go in.

• A good true golf story: I was at the Masters the year Nicklaus won his last one. I was sitting on sixteen, behind three guys from New York or Ohio or New Jersey. All I know is that they talked funny, and when Nicklaus's tee shot on the par three almost went in, stopping eight inches short of the flag, one of them said, "Never up, never in, Jack," and his fellow honkers laughed mightily.

Later, I went to get a beer. I noticed the four guys on the other side of the concession hut. One of them looked at the posted menu and said, "A Masters' sandwich, huh? That really sounds tip-top, guys."

Then he asked the young girl behind the counter, "What's in a Masters' sandwich?"

She answered with a very Southern, "Thar's ham, turkey, roast beef, cheese and ma-naise."

"Super. We'll have four Masters' sandwiches."

To which the girl replied, "We ain't got no more."

• My favorite golf balls: Slazengers. I like the package they come in.

• My favorite kind of golf shirts: Slazengers.

• Why I mentioned those two things: Maybe Slazenger will send me some free golf balls and shirts.

• A Ben Hogan story: Hogan was sitting in a locker room before a round, looking at golf balls with a magnifying glass.

Somebody asked him what he was doing.

"I'm throwing out the balls that have excess paint in the dimples," he answered.

• Most gentlemanly pro I ever played with: Dow Finsterwald. He also used only twenty-eight putts in the round.

• Best golf cartoon: Two guys are on a green. In the background is a large city. A nuclear bomb has sent a mushroom cloud rising above it. Says one guy to the other, "Go ahead and putt out. It'll be another four seconds before the shock wave hits."

• An absolute must read if you like golf: Besides this book, of course, don't miss *Dr. Golf*, by William Price Fox.

• Why restrooms on golf courses wouldn't be necessary except that women play occasionally: A man, when given a choice, will always take a leak outside rather than inside.

• What not to do when it begins to lightning on a golf course: Hold up a one-iron and say, "Even God can't hit this!" God is tired of hearing that story.

• One of the few things I would enjoy more than shooting a par round: Being naked with Kim Basinger in a sand trap at Pine Valley.

• Best recent golf rumor that probably isn't true: Nicklaus has trouble managing his money.

• Best tort and retort I've heard: "If I had your swing and my brain, I'd be on the tour."

"Yeah, and if I had your swing and you had a feather up your butt, we'd both be tickled."

• If there was one more Masters story to be written, who I'd like to see write it: Dan Jenkins or Furman Bisher.

• Somebody once asked me if I were really a redneck and what I replied: "Yes, but that's a four-iron in the gun rack of my truck."

• Something I've never understood: What's a "trace," and why does that word show up in names of new golf courses with a lot of expensive home sites?

• What American golf courses need: Names for each hole like they have in Scotland.

At Ansley Golf Club in Atlanta, an attractive nine-hole course that is a mean test of urban golf, I actually have named each hole. Here are the names and why:

No. 1: State Farm. That's because if you slice the ball off the first tee, it winds up on Montgomery Ferry Drive, and as soon as your insurance agent gets off the golf course, he'll have a message to call the irate owner of the new Saab that you hit.

No. 2: AIDS. Clear Creek runs across No. 2. Clear Creek isn't clear clean, however. The city found a bunch of used syringes in Clear Creek and put up a sign on it at Ansley that declares it a health hazard.

No. 3: Wino. To get to the par three third hole, you have to drive by a railroad underpass where a lot of winos sleep.

No. 4: Seaboard Coast Line. There are railroad tracks on the right of No. 4, and once I hit a shot that hit a passing freight train and it bounced off a Fruit Growers' Express car and onto the green and landed four feet from the pin where I made birdie.

No. 5: The Road Hole. You tee off about an 8-iron from Interstate 85.

No. 6: Greg Norman. If you hit the ball to the right side of the fairway, it can hit the cart path and roll all the way to the hole, four hundred yards away.

No. 7: Dammit All to Hell. What everybody says when they try to carry the lake in front of the green and don't make it.

No. 8: Halter Top: For the woman who lives in the house behind the green.

No. 9: The Pool Hole. They had to put up a big screen on the left side of the hole, a par three, because people were all the time hooking their shots into the pool. One day somebody in the men's grill asked, "Any good looking women out by the pool?"

An older gentleman replied, "I haven't looked today, but there haven't been any in seventy-six years."

• My last words: No, I can't get you two tickets for the Masters.

Golf Lingo

A glossary of golfing terms:

Addressing the ball – Be sure to use zip codes for prompt delivery. Or, "Hello, I'm Lewis, and I'll be your driver."

Caddy – A person paid to lose balls for others and find them for himself.

Chili-dip – A shot that goes half as far as you intended it to go, or a party dip that goes half as far as you intended it to go.

Divot – A flying carpet.

Drive – An afternoon spin, usually to the left or right, through a scenic, heavily wooded area.

Flag – A rallying point where players meet every twenty minutes or so to exchange alibis.

Fore! – The golf equivalent of an air-raid siren. When you hear it, fall flat with your face down and cover the back of your neck with your hands.

Gimmee – An uneasy agreement between players who can't putt.

Green – An area covered by a special grass that prevents balls from traveling in a straight line.

Handicap – A device for collective bargaining.

Improving your lie – Your wife didn't believe the first one, so you embellish it and try again.

Missing the cut – After being caught in the act of cheating, you outran the guy chasing you with a knife.

Par – Mathematical perfection, usually attained with a soft pencil and a softer conscience.

Put a good move on the ball – "What's your sign?" or, "Haven't we met somewhere before?" Also swinging properly.

Score – A fable in eighteen chapters.

Mixed scramble – A kinky breakfast.

Tee time – The last moment when golfers are seen laughing and joking.

Shot-gun start – A lot like a shot-gun wedding: you do it out of sequence and stroke it before you're ready.

Golf Clichés

What they really mean:

"Get it close." – Don't even think about making that putt.

"Good roll." – You didn't, and I'm delighted.

"Hold your head up." – If that sucker doesn't stop slicing soon, it'll land in Bulgaria.

"That'll play." – It ain't in the rough.

"Hit it, Alice." – Sexist remark for, "You left the putt short."

"Does your husband play golf?" – Same as above.

"All I had to do was hit it." – You left the putt an inch short, square in the hole. Your partner gives you half of the peace sign.

"Never up, never in." – Short again. Also the motto of the National Society of Impotence.

"Giraffe's ass shot." – High and stinky.

"That one leaked on you." – More like gushed.

"I'll take it if you want to hit another." – Stop your bitching. That's the best shot you've hit in a month.

"That dog'll hunt." – A keeper.

"Ain't no pictures on the scorecard." – It doesn't matter that it ricocheted off a rake before it bounced in the hole.

"Anything that travels that far ought to have a stewardess on board." – Compliment for a long drive.

"That one air-mailed me." – A drive that flies past an earlier one.

"Air-mailed to the wrong address." – An errant long drive, usually followed by snickering.

"That one took a victory lap." – A putt that circled the hole before falling in.

"How did it stay out?" – I know I missed the hole, but why didn't the wind blow it in?

"That's a teen-age putt." – It exploded in your hands.

"There's an Oral Roberts ball." – Shot hit off the heel of the club.

"You're playing Catholic golf – cross over here, cross over there." – Comment after a player chips back and forth over the green several times.

"That's a Baptist ball." – One that disappears under the water.

"That's a Methodist shot." – One that skips over it.

"You're playing Army golf – left, right, left, right." – Hitting it all over the golf course.

"Got enough club?" – Question asked of man urinating in the woods.

"Damn, this water is cold." – Spoken by man urinating into stream from the bank.

"Deep, too." – Spoken by man beside him who doesn't want to be outdone.